HOUSE OF TIDES

Kenneth White's work published in English

First period, 1966–1968
(published by Jonathan Cape, London)
The Cold Wind of Dawn, poems, 1966.
Letters from Gourgounel, narrative, 1966.
The Most Difficult Area, poems, 1968.

Second period, since 1989
The Bird Path, collected longer poems, Mainstream Publishing, Edinburgh and London, 1989, also in Penguin paperback edition, 1989.
Travels in the Drifting Dawn, narrative, Mainstream Publishing, Edinburgh and London, 1989, also in Penguin paperback edition, 1989.
Handbook for the Diamond Country, collected shorter poems, Mainstream Publishing, Edinburgh and London, 1990.
The Blue Road, narrative, Mainstream Publishing, Edinburgh and London, 1990.
Pilgrim of the Void, narrative, Mainstream Publishing, Edinburgh and London, 1992.
Van Gogh and Kenneth White, an encounter, Flohic Editions, Paris, 1994.
Coast to Coast, interviews, Open World Editions and Mythic Horse Press, Glasgow, 1996.
On Scottish Ground, selected essays, Polygon, Edinburgh, 1998.

Into the White World, two cassettes of poem readings, 1992.
Available from: Scotsoun, 13 Ashton Road, Glasgow G12 8SP.

The paradox of White's situation is that his work, written in English, with the exception of the essays mostly written in French, has appeared in French, and, substantially, in other languages, before it has appeared in English. With the ongoing publication of White's work in English, the paradox is diminishing, but it is still there. For a more complete bibliography of White's work, the only complete one being in French, see at the back of this book.

HOUSE
OF
TIDES

LETTERS FROM BRITTANY AND
OTHER LANDS OF THE WEST

KENNETH WHITE

Polygon

Polygon
An imprint of Edinburgh University Press Ltd
22 George Square, Edinburgh

Typeset in Weiss
by Hewer Text Ltd, Edinburgh, and
printed and bound in Great Britain by
Bell & Bain Ltd, Glasgow

A CIP record for this book is available
from the British Library

ISBN 0 7486 6279 0 (paperback)

The Publisher acknowledges subsidy from

THE SCOTTISH ARTS COUNCIL

towards the publication of this volume.

CONTENTS

Prologue   1

The Little Town of Lannion   7

Into Trébeurden   17

Neighbours   26

The Armorican Year   34

An Atlantic Studio   43

A Bibliophile Fantasia   51

The Paths of Stone and Wind   59

A Garden   72

The Great World of Little Catou   79

The Letter-box   89

From Plato to Plankton   98

Visitors   103

Echoes of Scotland   123

Listening to the Voices   129

Evening's Little Images   137

The Icelanders   143

An Old Owl's Nest   151

On the Ramparts of St Malo   155

Along the Margins   159

On the Paris–Brest   168

Memories of Kerouac   174

Brest, Bangkok and the Humpback Whale   180

September on Ushant   186

Season's End at Huelgoat   193

At the Hospital   202

Up through Late Britain   213

The Irish Jaunt   224

A Trip to the West Country   234

'The supreme degree of individualism is attained when, in the midst of total confusion, somebody founds his hermit kingdom.'
(Nietzsche)

'The kind of intellectual, mystic, imaginative life that Pelagius lived.'
(John Cowper Powys)

'How to find the North now? The North? Now? Over there, I think. Ah, here's the house.'
(William Carlos Williams)

'The restoration of the human house.'
(Charles Olson)

'There I was more myself and yet more strange.'
(Wallace Stevens)

'If you wish to know my real name, you must follow the road I took, you must try to see what I go back to.'
(Nô play, *Tamura*)

'It is on record that Kakei loved to paint the coast views of the tide flowing into the Kientang estuary.'
(Fenollosa)

PROLOGUE

In a general way, it's the Atlantic that governs our territory, creating the weather, shaping the coasts, wavelengthing minds.

The ocean-sea in these parts has three main channels: St George's, between England and Ireland; the Bristol Channel, between England and Wales; and the English Channel, which the French call *La Manche*, between England and France. At one time, not so long ago, those straits were tongues of ice that put a boreal chill into our waters, and they're still deeply in touch with the Arctic. But nowadays, the local sea-ways are fed also by the lukewarm upper waters of the Atlantic that come from tropical America.

It's a strange sea, the Celtic Sea (I'm using the term in a large sense), with its rocks, mists and sandbanks that appear and disappear: great humpbacked whales of sand, underwater pyramids of sand, whole cities of sand that can at times emerge above the surface before being wafted away again by the current. The flood-tide comes from the south and is not very strong. Stronger is the ebb-tide that flows from the gulfs and bays towards the south and south-east, causing the sands to migrate in that direction. Especially in its outer sections, where it is not protected by the tip of Ireland, the Celtic Sea is influenced also by long rollers coming ultimately from Labrador. In winter, polar depressions can raise violent storms and winds, generally westerly. Which is maybe one of the reasons (another being the ragged, jagged topography) for sea-folk sayings such as this:

Etre Pempoull ha Lokemo
emañ gwele an Anko

– 'Between Paimpol and Locquémeau lies the long bed of death.'

There's a death-obsession at this point of the setting sun, no doubt about it, and it has been much exploited in tale and legend over the centuries. But there is also something else, harder to define. Was it not one of the original philosophers who said: 'There are three types of men – the living, the dead, and those who sail upon the sea'?

I have been saying unashamedly, in passing, 'our' sea, 'our' waters. That's because for ten years now I have been living in the vicinity of a little port on the north coast of Brittany.

I'd written to a painter-friend, a native of the area: 'If ever you come across an old pirate's nest up there on the north coast, let me know.' I'd made that remark more or less in the air. We were living then, Marie-Claude and I, at Pau, in an apartment that looked out over a long range of the Pyrenees, from the Pic du Midi de Bigorre to the Pic d'Anie. It was a fine place, and the living, down there in the south-west, was good. But it *was* only an apartment, in a big high-rise building, and we were beginning to think in terms of a house, a real down-to-earth house of wood or stone somewhere. Seeing that 'somewhere' as near the sea, on the coast, we thought vaguely of the Basque country, or the pinelands of the Landes . . . But there was no rush. And then I'd made the acquaintance of the painter who lived in Brittany, and that rocky promontory, that outflung headland, suddenly seemed a better idea. So I'd put that remark to him, not really caring much if nothing ever came of it. But only three weeks later, back came the answer: 'I think I've maybe found it.'

We went up to see.

Imagine three stony buildings, one of them half-ruined, forming a triangle, on the heights above the village of Trébeurden. As you came through the gateway, you had on the left the first building, which consisted of three compartments, one a tool-shed, one a store-room, one a pigsty, rising one slightly above the other and in a slightly uneven line. The pigsty was in fact the original house (going back to the early eighteenth century). Next to that was a sturdy wide-doored building, with a stable on the ground floor and a granary on the top. And then, a bit higher than the other two buildings, stood the modern dwelling-house. At that time, it had two rooms on the first floor and a loft.

We began to imagine how we might live in it . . . decided we would . . . signed the papers.

Certainly it wasn't without qualms that we were going to be leaving the quiet warmth of Aquitania. I felt something like a Chinaman leaving the delights of southern, magnolia-suave Cathay for the wind-blown wilds of Mongolia. But, yes, I'd follow the dark meandering of the Amur river, I'd come to know in depth the Maritime Provinces. And I liked the idea of a kind of austere hermitage on a headland. While the work of renovation was going on at the house, I got a card from a Celtic scholar living near Trébeurden saying that he'd dropped by our place and that it looked, under a fall of snow, for all the world like *candida casa*, that monastery built by Ninian fourteen centuries ago, in Scotland. He knew what to say to please me, that fellow.

I was very well aware, of course, what I was exposing myself to by settling in Brittany. A lot of people would be saying not only that the 'intellectual nomad' I had talked so much about was turning sedentary, but that the Scottish writer was 'returning to his roots', maybe even on the hunt for korrigans or other local specialities of the sort. Well, with regard to 'what is said', I have come to think more and more in the terms of the old Scottish phrase: 'They say, they say – let them say.' But maybe, in these first pages, I should insist on the fact and make it crystal-clear that it wasn't identity I was after (which doesn't mean that some of the more subtle elements of Celtic culture won't be in the offing), it was a field of energy.

Maybe also a front: a *pelagic* front. You find those pelagic fronts all over the world – there's one in Japan (in the Kuroshio/Oyashio area), there's one south of Australia, there's one between Spain and Morocco. But there are some very interesting ones in this area of ours: there's the shelf front of the Bay of Biscay and the Celtic Sea, and, closer to hand still, the Ushant tidal front. A front is a place where waters of various types mix, a place of wild dynamics. It's also a place where life is abundant: fish life and plankton life flourish there. A few weeks ago, a friend sent me a photo taken by a satellite of phytoplankton blooms spotted just off the tip of Brittany, exceptional in extent. They are strangely beautiful: luminous biomasses eddying in a night obscurity.

I remember, during the first days of residence here, I had occasion to phone to Paris and, not getting in touch with the person intended, left my number with a secretary. 'Ah, that must be in the provinces?'

'No, madam, it's in Brittany.' Don't see that as local chauvinism. If I loathe supercilious centralism, I hate just as much localist couthiness: it's open space and concentrated place I go for. What had flashed and echoed in my brain at the time of that phonecall was a phrase or two from Pierre MacOrlan's *The Storm Lantern*, which I'd read down in Pau: 'When I think of the Brittany I love, the way I love things conducive to a certain fineness of mind, I like to think that a lot still remains to be said about this much-praised region. It's when you've been around France, around Europe, around the world, that you can begin to have an insight into Brittany's luminous secrets.' And then there was this, from Thoreau's *Cape Cod*, concerning the idea of an *Atlantic house*: 'The true Atlantic House, where the ocean is landlord as well as sealord'.

I have come to love with something more than love the windy shores and the rainy lanes of this place, where the country paths smell of seaweed and where the waves reflect the flowers of the yellow whin.

But before getting out on the roads, making acquaintance with the territory, seeing into the whole space, let's take another look at the house itself, and in particular what I was going to think of as my 'cosmopoetic laboratory'.

Outwardly, the buildings have not changed much since that day we first saw them. The windows are still the same size, though they now have aluminium frames, and there are some extra ones on the roof: more light! The outhouses are still covered in orange tiles, while the living house bears blue slates – a juxtaposition that is typical of this part of Brittany. And the great, sagging stable-door has been replaced by a sliding door-window of glass. But apart from that, and the garden, all the changes are on the inside, and there, they have been radical. The two lower rooms of the main dwelling-house have been transformed into one long, spacious room, and to it has been added an annexe that is the kitchen, and there are now two rooms in what was the loft, and a bathroom above the kitchen. The stable has been turned into a library, and the granary with its two skylights has become my writing-room. The tool-shed is still the tool-shed, the store-room has remained a store-room, and the pigsty has turned into a 'summer-house': a quiet, cool place – with no phone.

When, after about twelve months, all the necessary changes had been made, it was time to give the place a name.

We decided to call it Gwenved.

That is an old Celtic word which, in Christian texts, translates the notion of paradise. But it antedates Christianity by far. Literally 'white land', it indicates a place of light and concentration. In the *Triads of the Isle of Britain*, one reads: 'Three things the soul will find in the circle of Gwenved: primal power, primal memory, primal love.'

It sounded like an excellent programme.

This is the story, the ongoing story, of the place and the plan.

Works and days.

THE LITTLE
TOWN OF LANNION

Since Lannion is our main landmark, it's perhaps best to begin there.

For my vision of Lannion, no doubt the place to start from is the station – it's the spot in town I frequent the most.

Lannion station is a small, a very small station, tying up with Plouaret, where the fast trains stop that link Paris to Brest. Built of brick, it is painted yellow on the outside and is decorated inside with photographs of the coast. A little green *micheline* train is usually seen parked back of it, and in front of it stands the *Hôtel de Bretagne*, and, next to it, *Le Graal*.

When you come out of the station at Lannion, and walk along the Rue du Général-de-Gaulle towards the town centre, you pass the *Bar de l'Ouest*. In the early days, I liked to sit in there, listening to what the people had to say. The only snag was that it was difficult to hear the talk because of the budgies: there was a huge cage of them in what had been the fireplace, and they raised one awful racket. I'd be straining my ears while staring at advertisements for *'Clacquesin, extrait des pins'* and *'Chocolat Van Houten'*. But I gradually began to use the Bar de l'Ouest for more solitary, meditative practices. I liked just to sit in there watching the gulls flying above the Sankt Anna bridge and over the river Léguer. Sometimes I had a book with me, and I remember one time it was *The River Sumida* by Nagai Kafu, containing, like all the books I love, phrases that lift the mind into a kind of eternity: 'As the light faded, the white of the gulls became whiter still. It was a sight to make a poet want to drink.' In memory of Kafu, I ordered a bottle of Muscadet and drank it slowly till the last gull had gone to rest. I liked the *Bar de l'Ouest*. I only gave up going to it when they installed a pin-ball machine, a lurid affair called Black Pyramid, made in Milwaukee. You would see treasure-hunters prancing madly across the screen, and hear now and then a burst of machine-gun fire . . .

Not far from the *Bar de l'Ouest* stood the *Bar de la Marine*. That was another place I frequented a lot those first days. I remember in particular one October evening. Humped over a glass of beer, Jude Le Breselec was telling tales of the old town and, while he was at it, expounding his social theories: 'There used to be two thousand seamen here, by God.' Most of them had not been fishermen, but merchant-navy men. He himself had been a merchant seaman: cargo ships and tankers. The offices of the Company were at Nantes, in the rue Jean-Bart, and his home port was Marseilles, but there were times when he had to join his ship at faraway places like Copenhagen or Hamburg. That meant a hell of a lot of gadding about, and he was never at home. In the end, fed up with the situation, his wife had delivered an ultimatum: 'Jude Le Breselec, it's the bosses or me.' 'Hell's bells,' thought Jude. After careful consideration, he decided it had better be his wife, and that the time had come to change jobs. So he took on road cargoes, becoming a truck driver. Along the roads, he noticed that roadside restaurants did pretty good business, so, after a couple of years' trucking, he decided to chuck the truck and open a 'workers' restaurant' in Lannion. 'Things weren't so easy then as they are now,' he said. 'Nowadays money falls from the sky, it's easy gold. But, it's true too, once you've got hold of a good job, you have to try and stick to it. In the old days, a boat of 14,000 tons had a crew of forty. Nowadays you can run a boat of 400,000 tons with twenty-four lads. Same thing on land. In the old days, to work ten or twenty acres took five men. Nowadays, one fellow alone can take on two hundred acres or more. You can't get by that fact: the machine kills man.'

Still within the station area, in the Bozuko quarter, stood (and still stands) the *Ty Krampouz* ('pancake-house') *St Christophe*. That was another place in Lannion I used to haunt. It looks old from the outside, with a mass of tousled, pale-blue virginia creeper over its arched and dark-stoned doorway, but it looks even older inside. As you enter the door, there's a bar on the left, but the crumpet-serving room is on the right, and it's very small and dark, with two massive, deeply-carved Breton cupboards leaving room only for two tables with benches and stools. If packed in, maybe a dozen people could be accommodated, but nobody would have to sneeze, especially if there was some slight person perched at the end of the bench. One afternoon, I was in there all alone. I'd come in and sat down at one of the tables, waiting for the old woman who was doing some cleaning at the bar to come through and ask me what I wanted. When she did, I said I'd like a coffee. It came in a little pot, and the cup and saucer beside it quaintly antique, with a dainty, rosy pattern of flowers. 'You can't sit there in the dark!' cried the old one, and stretched out her hand to the switch. 'Oh,' I said, 'I don't need any

light. I just want to sit here quiet for a while, but thanks all the same.'
'Well,' she said, 'if you want it, you know where it is.' When she'd
gone back to the bar, I let my eye rove round the room, which wasn't
really dark, just a little obscure, for the only window was very small
and a chintz curtain covered most of it. But enough light came in to
put a red-golden gleam on a large copper pan that sat in one corner –
like a salmon in the river.

There used to be salmon galore in the Léguer, and there still are a few.
But even if there are fewer fish in it, it's still good to have a river, and
quite a strong, rippling river running through the town. Certainly not
everybody feels it that way: some people think it's just a convenient
place to get rid of old tyres and even old beds, which you'll see
sticking up out of the mud at low tide. And one municipal councillor
had a dream, all his life, throughout all his long and meritorious
career, he had a dream: to endow his dear town with an aquatic
stadium where sporting enthusiasts might learn how to expertly
paddle a canoe and run races with them. He finally had it built a
few years ago, a thick and ugly contraption, between the Sankt Anna
bridge and the Kermaria bridge. One wishes, I know it's a hard thing
to say, that municipal councillors had no dreams . . .
　　There are three bridges over the Léguer at Lannion: the Pont
Kermaria, the Pont Ste Anne, just mentioned, and the Pont de
Viarmes. If you stand on the Pont de Viarmes facing upstream
and look up to the left, you see the church of Brelevenez. And if
you climb up the long flight of steps leading to that church, you get a
good overall view of the town. Unless, as happens, it's covered in
mist, in which case it will be reduced to a huddle of white gables
emerging ghostily from the greyness.

But it wouldn't do to equate Lannion with mists and ghosts. In fact,
it's quite a lively little place. In all the surrounding countryside, it has
always had a reputation for elegance and wit. Hence the saying: 'He's

from Lannion, gents, you can see that from the crease in his pants.' Le Goffic of Lannion achieved some literary distinction, ending up in the French Academy, if you please, and there was a writer who arrived at something more than distinction: I'm thinking of Villiers de l'Isle-Adam, author of *Axel, Le Testament d'un poète* ('A poet's testament') and *Le Nouveau Monde* ('The new world'), who, around 1846, lived at no. 14 on the Place du Marc'hallac'h. Also, many of the citizens of Lannion have been around the planet, picking up phenomena and information of all kinds that turn up here and there. One of the local dentists has a display of exotic teeth at the door to his waiting-room, all donated by local people: the head of a leopard with yellow fangs from Brazzaville, the jaw of a shark with magnificent rows of incisors from Abidjan . . .

Lannion today houses about twenty thousand souls.

If you stand on the Quai d'Aiguillon, with your back to the river, you have the post-office to your left, and, to your right, a supermarket called Festival. In between, going from left to right, I mean from west to east, you have the *Pharmacie de la Poste*, the *Banque Populaire d'Armorique*, the *Assurances Mutuelles Agricoles*, the *Crédit Maritime Mutuel*, a property agency, the local offices of the newspaper *Ouest-France*, a tearoom called *À la Brioche fine*, a *Centre Leclerc*, a boutique selling leather goods, an old furniture shop, *Meubles d'Art*, the offices of the *Electricité et Gaz de France*, the *Galeries d'Aiguillon*, another bank, the *Société Générale*, a shop selling household goods, a tobacco shop, and a shop selling ladies' underwear.

From the Quai d'Aiguillon, four streets lead up to the Place du Marc'hallac'h, two of them passing through the Place du Centre: the Avenue Ernest-Renan, which becomes the Rue Jeanne-d'Arc; the Rue St-Yves which passes by the church of St-Jean-du-Baly; the Rue Le Taillandier, which turns into the Rue du Miroir; and the Rue des Augustins, which turns first into the Rue Saint-Malo, then into the Rue des Chapeliers. Joining these streets there are little lanes and vennels, like the Venelle de l'Enfer ('Hell's Alley') and the Venelle des Trois Avocats ('The Three Lawyers' Lane'), as well as bigger streets like the Rue Duguesclin. At the corner of the Rue Duguesclin and the Rue Saint-Malo stands the *Comptoir des Indes,* a café with a thick red-daubed façade and a smoky, woody, dark interior. Parallel to the Rue Duguesclin is the Rue G.-de-Pontblanc, and there you'll find a little plaque on the grey granite wall bearing information about a gentleman who fought the English in the fourteenth century:

HERE

MET A HEROIC DEATH

DEFENDING

THE TOWN OF LANNION

AGAINST THE ENGLISH

SIR

GEOFFROY DE PONTBLANC

KNIGHT

1346

Market day in Lannion, which is a Thursday, is quite a busy and picturesque affair. It concerns not only the redbrick and green metal central market (*Halles Centrales*) on the Place du Miroir (*Plazenn ar Melezour*), with its horsemeat butcher, its cheese merchant, its fruit and vegetable sellers, its delicatessens and, close by, the fishmongers, but practically the whole town. The Quai d'Aiguillon is packed with stalls, so are the streets leading up to the Place du Centre and the Place du Marc'hallac'h. At one corner, a busker will be playing a flute, at another it will be a drum, at another spot again, bagpipes. You will recognise Breton, Irish and Scottish melodies, at times even a Peruvian rhythm. And somebody will be singing, one day or another:

> *There were two of us, there were three of us*
> *all from the isle of Groix and sailors*

blows the wind, blows the wind
the seawind that'll drive you out of your mind.

I like walking round the stalls, listening to the conversations. Here's one I overheard one day at the delicatessen's stall. A woman, elderly, is being served:

'You're not a Breton, you', she says to the pork-butcher.

'What makes you say that, lady?', says the fellow, jovial, but on the defensive, and ready to pounce.

'Your moustaches', says an elderly chap waiting behind the elderly woman. The pork-butcher is in fact sporting splendiferous handle-bars.

'My name is Jospin. Jospin, that's the way they say it here. At Carhaix, they say Jôpin. I don't know how they say it in Quimper. It changes from one valley to the other.'

'It's just the pronunciation that changes. It's always Breton', chips in another man.

'I've got a teaser for you,' says the butcher. 'How do you say "*jambon*" in Breton?'

The linguistically inclined man is a bit discountenanced:

'I used to know . . .', he murmurs.

It's the woman that comes to the rescue:

'We say *djambon*. We just bretonise the French a bit,' she says.

'See what I mean?', says the butcher.

It may not be too obvious to the recent incomer exactly what the butcher wants his clients to see, but it's all about language and identity, and there's a latent debate going on between cosmopolitanism and localism.

I move around all the stalls and stands, but it's mainly the fish-stalls I'm attracted to, with their flat oysters and their curved oysters, their shrimps and their scallops, their spider-crabs and their sleeper-crabs, their salmon and their sardines, their pollacks and their bass, their sand-eels and their wrasse, their gurnards and their red mullet. I saw one day what looked like extra-big gurnards and asked where they were fished. Oh, but they're not gurnards, I was told, they're a cousin of the gurnard, called *mouline* – their fins, you see, are dark-blue-green, whereas those of the gurnard are rosy-red. Oh yes, I said, I saw.

At the end of the nineteenth century, there were about two hundred boats fishing out of Lannion. That wasn't an awful lot, compared with five hundred at Paimpol, six hundred at Audierne, and seven hundred at Concarneau. But it was a lot compared with now, when there are hardly more than half-a-dozen. That said, there's still a fishing instinct in the people. At the time of the big tides, a kind of glee comes over the population. On those days, you might find it hard to get your tyre repaired or your tap fixed. Some folk just don't turn up for work at all. They're out on the shore, raking away like crazy for clams and hunting about for abalones.

As it passes through Lannion, the Léguer, as I've indicated, is for most folk only environment, decor, even dump. But as from the Quai de la Corderie, it comes again into its own, it enters into its own secret life.

I suggest we follow the river now down to Lannion Bay.

If you walk past the post-office, past the bridge of Viarmes, along the Avenue de la Résistance, you come to the beginning of the old rope-makers' quay. There's an old hulk moored on the left bank of the river at that point, an old hulk overgrown with grass but still masted. On the top of the mast, maybe twenty feet high, you'll often see a cormorant, black and still – like a totem.

Let's come to one particular day . . .

All quiet on the Quai de la Corderie. Houses line the bank, and, curious to see how people live in them, how they're laid out and arranged, I look in. In one, I see a pile of knitting on a table; in another, a model ship with blue sails. And I'm just getting my eye adjusted to the obscurity of another when a woman comes to the window and, very forcibly, very ostensibly, to make sure I get the message, draws the curtain tightly close.

Anyway, it's the river I'm really interested in.

A little farther on from the lone totem-cormorant, I come across a nervous band of gulls, now riding the brown waters, now fluttering up for a quick jaunt, then settling down again, but with watchful eyes. Farther on still, on a gravelly sand-spit, five cormorants are grouped together, absolutely still, like their mast-top mate, looking into the rain that has begun to fall and seeing I wonder what. I take shelter under an overhanging rock-face, more to enter into touch with the rock than to take shelter, and watch the cormorants for a while. Not a move do they make, even when a jogger plods and pants by in a bright-pink tracksuit.

I'm glad the rain has begun to fall, nippling and spreading little circles on the river's brown waters. It makes the atmosphere more intimate, increases the loneliness, gives more density to the space.

The cormorants still haven't moved. I keep my eyes on them for a few minutes longer, wishing I'd brought my binoculars with me, so as to be closer to them, so as maybe to see into their eyes, or see the wind ruffling the feathers of their necks, but not regretting the absence of the binoculars too much, thinking that it's just as well to be there as I am, and that inner vision will amply compensate for the lack of ocular precision.

I start walking into the rain again, past the red-hulled *Sir Cedric* from Paimpol, berthed at a pier beside a huge pile of sand. A crane is biting into that sand-pile and building up a second pile alongside it. I see no human being: only the pier, and the ship, and the piles of sand, and the crane moving with a faint *clank-clunk, clank-clunk.*

It's a few hundred yards farther along the path that I see the heron, a grey heron, as still as the cormorants if not stiller – head poised, beak pointed into the air. It is standing on the bank opposite, on a field of grass, grey against the discreet green, grey under the grey sky, still as a stone: sheer beauty, perfect presence.

I don't want to look too much, or say too much (even to myself), I just keep walking, with the grey heron in the corner of my eye, in a corner of my mind.

My own house is very near the mouth of the Léguer. If my postal address is '22560 Trébeurden', I live in fact about four kilometres from the village, which is to say about seven kilometres from Lannion, just after that place on the Lannion road called 'the white field', because when there's frost, that's where it starts. In the old days, when the frost came, the folk would say: 'The white wolf crossed the field this morning.'

Into Trébeurden

I n my early days here, I read in a little brochure put out by some local institution that Trébeurden meant 'the place of Brandan', after the name of the Irish peregrine monk whose traces I had followed assiduously over the years in Ireland and in the Western Isles, and who was certainly in these parts at one time (there's a village called Brandan just a few miles away), maybe paying a visit to his co-mate in marginal Christianity and in erratic navigation, St Malo. But that was too good to be true. In fact, Trébeurden means 'The place (*tré* is an ecclesiastic district, like *plou* and *lan*) of the Britons'. Which is after all just as interesting, maybe more so, since it would seem to indicate that Trébeurden was one of the first places where the insular Bretons (or Britons) landed and settled in the troubled times of the trans-channel migrations.

You have to imagine some Irish, Welsh or Scottish monks, eager to get away from Anglo-Saxon molestations and vulgarities, setting out in the fifth and sixth centuries, with some companions in a small boat and trusting to 'the winds of God', as they put it, to take them to a better place. They'd be travelling days and nights on end, over the choppy waves, through the meandering mists, and then one morning they'd spy new land: a curving, misty coastline, where they'd beach their boat, bless the Lord, and get down to building some solid shelters. The boat they'd usually leave to rot on the beach. Now, in the bottom of those boats they'd had a big flat stone for cooking on. And when the wood of the boat had rotted away, all that remained was the stone. So the story would go about among the locals that those strange fellows had crossed the sea on stone boats . . .

That was Trébeurden at the beginning: those travelling monks, lay folk with them at the time, or a little later. Gradually, they would set up a parish, a saintly little place on the coast now inhabited by fishers of fish and fishers of men.

With all that in mind, let's leap up a few centuries of fishing and preaching, and come to more modern days.

By the beginning of the twentieth century, Trébeurden had turned into a quiet little hyperborean Biarritz, frequented in the summer by a metropolitan and cosmopolitan crowd out for the wild scenery, the invigorating sea-baths, and up to all kinds of high jinks. You hear tales about Slavonic countesses dancing stark naked on the beach, and of local girls getting married to princes from Mitteleuropa.

In July or early August, the Daimlers and Bugattis would leave the posher districts of Paris and the families would take up residence in their summer quarters, at Trébeurden by the sea.

Here's what the 1911 edition of the *Guide Joanne* (I picked it up in a second-hand bookshop in Lannion) had to say:

'Of the departments formed out of the ancient Province of Brittany, the Côtes-du-Nord has been even further removed from the general movement of history than the Morbihan or the Finistère . . . The climate of the Côtes-du-Nord is one of the most temperate in France, not because of its latitude, but because of its proximity to the sea, which keeps temperatures even and warm. This privileged department is part of a peninsula, and if it is washed by the Channel, it also receives beneficial rains from the nearby ocean. Almost all of its valleys are deep, wild and winding, and its shores offer some of the most beautiful views that man can contemplate on this earth.'

That was not only attractive, it was true, and still is. So in they swarmed, from Paris, from the rest of France, from all over Europe, from the Americas. Those were the hey-days of Trébeurden.

In winter, 'the season' over, quietness would descend again, and the little burg would be returned to the gulls and the fisherfolk.

When I first settled at Trébeurden, I was in touch with the latter-day remnants of that Trébeurden summer society. In one of those 'high society' houses, there was a very elegant and charming Italian who had been in the publishing business in Milan. He told me a story about Hemingway and Faulkner (you remember those American novelists who made a lot of noise in the early twentieth century?). A literary critic of his acquaintance had interviewed Hemingway over a bottle of chianti and, in the latter stages of their talk, had come out with a bold and pernicious question: 'Do you think you're better than Faulkner?' Hemingway paused for a second: 'No,' he said finally, 'Faulkner's better than me – I get drunk as from six o'clock, he starts at two.' Then there was the lady who'd spent a very gay youth among galant army officers in North Africa – love among the dunes, and all that kind of thing. She wanted me to come and turn tables in her house, 'like Victor Hugo in Guernesey'. In fact, if *I* turned up, she flatteringly added, maybe Hugo himself would pay us a visit. I declined the invitation.

If you come into Trébeurden from the Lannion road, you find first of all a little centre consisting of church (in a niche, a saint with a gull shitting ritually on his head), post-office, *mairie* (it'll sport defiantly a Breton black-and-white flag beside the Jacobine tricolour, and recently has added the flag of United Europe), a shop or two, a pancake-house, a couple of cafés (one with a big poster: *yehed mad*, 'good health'), as well as a couple of banks. Then the long, long Rue de la Plage runs down to lower Trébeurden, past chunky houses of grey or red granite bearing names like *Ker Nelly, Ker Nathalie, Ker Yvonne*, all neat and often flowered, with gardens full of contorted apple-trees and creamy-smooth camelias. At the foot of the Rue de la Plage, you have another centre: a restaurant, *Le P'tit Resto*; a garage, *Le P'tit Garage*; a butcher's shop ('takeaway buckwheat cakes'); a second post-office . . . And then there's the Rue de Trozoul, steep, and in its second half tunnelled deep out of the rock, running down to the harbour. Away down at the bottom stands the hotel *Ker an Nod*, on the terrace of which I used to like to sit those first days, looking out over the bay.

My first acquaintance with Trébeurden was at a dinner organised here by that painter-friend I mentioned, Gildas Gouazic, one evening in the late spring of 1983. Gildas had arranged everything in advance with Brigitte the proprietrix: the lobster was delicious, the wine was excellent, and the company, congenial. Christophe Le Foll was there, and the two Tanguy brothers with their wives. Stories went the round. Gildas had been in the insurance business before he became a painter, and he told the incident of the man trying to sell life insurance at a local farm. The agent had explained at great length his mission to the farmer, the farmer had dutifully called out to his wife: 'Rozen, here's the Death Insurance folk!', and the wife had cried back: 'Tell the buggers to go to hell!' Then, somebody had just come back from Ireland and he had the story about the Ulster constabulary man who ascends to heaven. The constable goes up to St Peter and states his identity. 'Oh, but we can't let you in here', says St Peter, 'with all the terrible crimes you have on your hands and all you've done against our poor IRA boys.' 'I'm not wantin' in your place at all', says the Ulster man. 'I'm only here to tell you people you have five minutes flat to vacate the premises.'

It was a pleasant evening, but what I remember most was the stupendous sunset: the great red mass of the sun behind a clump of dark-green pine. It was like something out of a Japanese floating world print. This 'Japanese feeling' was to come over me again and again on the coast. It's maybe something to do with the configuration of the land and the weather, and a Japanese painter-friend here on a visit has confirmed this. The weather, by the way, often changes between Lannion and Trébeurden. In winter, while the mist is thick over Lannion, there may be sun on the coast and the sky opalescent, like the inside of an illuminated oyster. In summer, it's the opposite: the coast can be wrapped in mist, while Lannion is clear and the sun shining.

Just in front of the hotel *Ker an Nod* stands a monument to the memory of the politician Aristide Briand, one of the lights of the Third Republic, a minister of the government twenty-five times, a prophet of peace ('Down with rifles, machine-guns, cannon. Up with peace, reconciliation, discussion!'), and who, away back there in 1930, was already speaking of a Federal Union of Europe. Briand was often in Trébeurden. He'd come here from the tensions and stresses of Paris to visit his mistress, whose house, now in ruins, rises there conspicuous on the little island of Millau, named after one of those saintly sea-folk in the coracles, a certain Milio. While we salute Briand, and listen to stories about those obstreperous and supposedly licentious parties on the once saintly island, let's think even more of the man who for long was Briand's secretary, Alexis Léger. Léger, better known to the world as Saint-John Perse, was probably the greatest French poet of the twentieth century. I'd come across the tracks of Saint-John Perse in Pau, where he'd lived as a young man, then later on in Guadeloupe, where he was born, and it was strange for me to pick up thoses traces again here. Back from his war exile in America, Saint-John Perse had thought of settling in Brittany, on an island. Before a plutocratic American admirer offered him a place on the coast of Provence, it was that very island of Millau he had had his eye and heart on.

During our early days in Trébeurden, while work was going on at the house, Marie-Claude and I lived in a little studio on the edge of one of Trébeurden's beaches: Tresmeur ('the big beach'). At that time, when I was still trying to get my bearings, I used to frequent the cafés. I'd try them all, for the atmosphere and the conversation. The one I went to most often was the *Coup d'Roulis* ('The rolling ocean').

I remember the first morning I was in there.

It would be about eleven o'clock. I'd been on my own for an hour or so, but in came now a chap about fifty years old, with a sailor's cap on his head:

'Mornin'!'

A glass of red wine, same as usual, is set before him on the counter.

'Looks grim, eh?', says the barman.

'Aye.'

'Think it'll lift?'

'Maybe.'

'Is the glass risin'?'

'No . . . Well, a bit.'

End of conversation.

The sailor-man sips his wine in a truly cosmic silence.

Then, abruptly:

'Right, I'll away.'

This, I felt, was Brittany.

Another time, back in the *Coup d'Roulis*, Yves Cadiou was telling about a wild trip he'd made between Perros and St Malo: 'There was a strong northerner blowing. We were soaked to the skin.' For some reason or other which I didn't catch, one of the crew on arriving at St Malo was *'tout zébédéné'*. I'd noted the unfamiliar word, and later asked Yves what it meant. *'Zébédéné, zébédéné'*, he said, 'it means astonished, flabbergasted'. He went on to say it was local usage and probably came from Zebedee, the father of James and John, who was all surprised when Christ turned up out of the blue asking his sons to be 'fishers of men'. Another time – that would have been 14 July – I heard this from a burly fellow in a sailor's jersey drinking with his mates in a corner: 'It was the French that stormed the Bastille, not the Bretons Anyway maybe we're really all Vikings . . . Shit, there I've got myself drunk again.' And it was in the *Coup d'Roulis* that a man sat down next to me, asking if I was on holiday:

'No', I said, 'I live here.'

'But anyone can see by your accent that you're not from here.'

Dammit, I thought – is my Scottish-English showing? That *can* happen now and then when I'm tired. But the man went on to say:

'Anybody can see you're from the south.'

So it wasn't after all my Scottish-English that was showing, it was my seventeen years in the south-west. I was reassured; I was positively pleased.

One morning, all the talk in the *Coup d'Roulis* was about the change of the department's name from the Côtes-du-Nord (*Aodou an Hanternoz*, in Breton), the north coast, to the Côtes-d'Armor, the Sea Coast. North, it seemed, was bad for publicity. It made the public think of ice and fog and chill remoteness, whereas what you need for the tourist industry, as every advertiser knows, is eternally blue sky and an unfailing, unblinking sun. So the long-fought political-cultural-touristic campaign for a change of name had reached a triumphant conclusion. Henceforth, we would not be 'The Coasts of the North', but 'The Coasts of the Sea'. On the morning of which I'm thinking, reactions in the *Coup d'Roulis* were diverse. For some, plunged in their rolling deep-blue dreams, the only response to this resounding news was a laconic, monosyllabic 'humph'. Others thought it was too damn' close to Côte d'Azur. As for Roparz, 'at least it's Breton', he said. 'Like the Morbihan', said Goulven. 'What's the Finistère?', asked Pol. 'It's Latin,' said somebody. I was thinking to myself that 'coasts of the sea' was a bit pleonastic. But after all, that's no uncommon thing in common usage. In the Meuse area, you've got a place called Montblainville, and there you have 'mountain' twice, the *blain* coming from a Celtic word meaning 'height' (*blein*, in Breton). The same goes for Montaigu-le-Blin in the Allier, and Montblin in the Seine-et-Marne. So we'll be able to live with Côtes d'Armor – so long, of course, as we keep a sense of the real magnetic points and don't forget, under all the hullaballoo of names, the real nodes of significance.

Those first days, I wandered quite a lot around Trébeurden, and I remember walking in its main street one night around midnight. It was raining, a windy salty rain, and a big yellow moon peaking over the horizon. Not a soul in sight. Then suddenly a man appeared on the church square and started shouting:

'We're not wild beasts! I'm telling you, and I'll tell you again. We're not wild beasts. Not at all!'

It was like the incarnation of some old Celto-Breton complex, the anguished expression of an accumulated misunderstanding . . .

When this 'ghost' had lurched off again into the darkness, I continued prowling round the streets, past the occasional lighted window.

When I got back home, I was looking round my study with quiet satisfaction, feeling the whole 'field' ready, when the phone rang. I picked up the receiver:

'Hallo?'

'You'll be my husband?'

'No madam, you've got the wrong number.'

'I love you, I love you, I love you!'

'Madam, you've got . . .'

'Are you coming tonight? Are you coming tonight?'

'Madam, as I've already said, you've got the wrong number.'

'Don't come that stuff with me, you dirty rat. I know you're there with some bitch.'

NEIGHBOURS

Our immediate neighbours on the Gwaker Road (*Gwaz-ker*, 'the hamlet by the stream'?) are the Alaniou, Pol and Aline. Pol is a cook on the Brittany ferries, doing the triangular run between Roscoff, Plymouth and Santander, at home one week, away the other. Aline is a secretary at a clinic in Lannion. Their two kids go to school at Trébeurden. Up back of us live the Rannou, who run a farm, growing maize, wheat and rye, sometimes colza, raising pigs and goats. They have three children, a boy and two girls, the eldest of whom is studying Latin and Greek at the university in Rennes. The general neighbourly atmosphere is very

Breton, which is to say discreet without being distant, inviting without being invading.

A few hundred yards down the road live the Thoraval. Monsieur Thoraval told me when I first met him that he was '17 – the wrong way round'. His is probably the longest memory in the district; his family has lived here for three centuries. It was he who told me that the old name of our house was Crech ar Forn, i.e. the Hill of the Oven, which probably means that at one time this was where bread was baked for the neighbourhood. At that first meeting, we were sitting in the Thoraval's big room, which at one time was a bar. Through the big window to the South, you could see a good stretch of the Finisterrian coast, with an apple-tree hiding the Île de Batz. Thoraval told me that when you hear the pebbles rolling on the beach at Beg Leguer, it's a sign of bad weather – same when the tide roars loud under a North wind on Lannion Bay. That's when the beasts are nervy, and his dog, Gina, goes into a corner. But most of the talk that day was about what Thoraval called *le whisky de la mer* ('sea-whisky'), that is, all those kegs of whisky that had been washed ashore in the winter of 1982 on the beaches of Trébeurden and Île-Grande, and which the people had appropriated under the noses of the customs officers. Invited to sample it (*'Yehed mad,'* said Thoraval), I found it pungent stuff, slightly salty. It made Thoraval want to sing. Declaring that he had a voice 'that could go through walls', he proceeded to demonstrate. He didn't like modern songs; they were all too lovey-dovey: *Je t'aime, je t'aime . . .* He didn't like the Marseillaise either, found it too nationalistic and bloody-minded. When they sang it at the Old Soldiers' Club, he would keep his arse stuck to the bench, with his gub shut tight. He preferred *Breiz ma bro*, which, he said, had the same tune as the anthem of the Welsh. After singing a bit of this, we had more talk. The other day, old man Thoraval said, he and some pals were out gathering mussels on the Île Millau. After the fishing, they were, naturally, thirsty, so they went over to the café *Les Roches Blanches*. They were nattering away among themselves, when a couple at a neighbouring table, who turned out to be Swiss, put a question to them, which led to the following conversation:

'What language is that you're talking?'

'Our mother tongue, naturally.'

'And what is your mother tongue?'

'Breton.'

'Oh, that's a dialect of French, isn't it?'

'No, to tell you the truth, French at its best is a dialect of Breton. French is what they speak in Paris. Breton is what they speak in paradise.'

Once they'd got the linguistic question worked out to their totally unscientific satisfaction, they began talking about the weather, which happened at that moment to be very fine. The Swiss had always heard that the Bretons lived perpetually stooped under umbrellas.

'Not quite, madam,', said Thoraval, 'sometimes we even get sunstroke.'

The Swiss were delighted to find such pleasant, sunburnt people.

'Are all the Bretons like you?' they said.

'No, I'm afraid not', said Thoraval, 'the others are better.'

Not far from the Thoraval lives Jean-Yves, who calls himself a real Parisian, since he was born, like his seven brothers and six sisters, at the Bichat hospital, in the eighteenth arrondissement. But his mother was a Finisterrian. He was an SDF (*sans domicile fixe* – 'no fixed abode') in Paris before he came to Trébeurden. Before that, he had been a labourer, then he did farm work in the Ardennes. They often came across cases of munitions (American rockets) in the woods there. His boss found a load one time, stacked them up against a tree – and then couldn't remember which tree it was: 'the foresters must have got their heads blown off'. He'd had a pal in Paris, twenty-five years old, who'd committed suicide by hanging himself, so depressed was he at being out of work. He himself had lived for a while with a girl, and then she'd died of a heart attack, at thirty-nine. That's when, completely shattered, he'd decided to come out to Brittany. He had worked at first as a municipal scavenger then as a gardener. He liked the life in Brittany, but found the winter a bit tough.

Another neighbour, a bit further afield (he lives over by Bégard) is the flute-player, Pol Kermarrech, who knows all about bamboo and who had just returned from years' living in Ireland when I met him first. That was at his parents' place, in Locarn, near Callac. His mother had prepared a meal of crumpets with buttermilk and afterwards we went for a walk along the Corong gorges, a chaos of boulders left by some ice-age torrent, and the water, brandy-brown, rushing among them. It was autumn, a chill red-gold marking the woods of oak and beech. Pol told me a hermit had lived in those woods up till recently, and that Locarn itself was originally a hermitage (Loc Carn, 'Carn's hermitage'). But what struck me most was what he said about the gorges themselves. His conjecture was that there must be very low sound-waves there, inaudible, but soothing to the nerves. I liked that idea of silent, but deeply satisfying music.

It was Kermarrech that introduced me to the potter who lives in the woods near Trémargat. He works a furnace of a model going back to sixth-century China, which he fires with wood, bringing it up to 1300°. You have to feed in the wood for hours, regulating the air intake. Erwan uses different kinds of wood and the cinders from the various woods give different effects, that he calls 'gifts of the fire': irregular blemishes that are seen as beauty spots. It was from him Marie-Claude bought the rough-grained tea-bowls we use.

The naturalist lives on the Kavan road. I first went to visit him with the body of a little tit that had banged itself to death against the kitchen window. He was working at a huge bird, a *nandou* from the pampas of Uruguay. Alive, the nandou is a big, long-legged creature with powerful muscles, able to run at great speed. Now it was a heap of tissue and feather steeping in a bucket before being set up again into a semblance of life. Even though its death was accidental, the naturalist said he couldn't do my little tomtit because it was on the protected list. We got then to talking about his profession. He said he'd done his apprenticeship in the Finistère. But he couldn't stay there. There are few taxidermists left, and they have few clients, so an established taxidermist will only teach the trade to someone who's willing to move to another area and not become a rival. Alain likes his job, loves to do pheasants, and has a whole collection of them. He pointed with some pride to a weasel he felt he'd made a good job of, since he hadn't destroyed the keenness of its sharp little face. As to the fox, it was hard to do, very hard to get its body movement and catch its expression. The one he showed me was the only one he was pleased with. He'd kept the skin preserved in the fridge for a long time, waiting for 'what artists call the state of grace'. That moment had come, and he'd done it. He spoke with quiet enthusiasm about the mandarin duck, how even after years it will try to escape from a farm. From June to September, losing its magnificent feathers, it goes all grey, gets very timid and hides away from the world. The waterhen will also try to escape. The one he showed me, black with a red beak, had managed to climb out of a wire cage where some people had tried to domesticate it, even going so far as to cut its wing feathers. But it had climbed out and, though it couldn't fly, had walked off and was killed on the road. This man was surrounded by dead animals, but they all had a fierce, live presence and I had a strange feeling in that cluttered room of his: chamber of death, tomb of eternal life. Which is maybe why I said to him that the fine thing about his job was that he was obliged to know a lot about *live* animals. 'Yes', he said, 'and you begin to ask more and more of yourself, you try to *live up to* the animals.'

The geographer lives in the little street of Saint-Yves in Lannion that runs up from the quays behind the church of St-Jean-du-Baly, whose bells can be heard from his study. I'd met him first in a local shop where he was having a photocopy made of a map he had just drawn: a 'panoceanic projection' of the world ocean. I'd said that looked very interesting. 'Ah', he said, 'at last somebody who finds what I do interesting!' Jean-Paul Duchamp's study looks down on to a wildered little garden full of crabby apple-trees and is packed with maps and books. But it's nothing compared to the attic. Up there, there's everything and anything, but all neatly arranged, including boxes labelled by his mother, who could never resign herself to throwing anything at all away. He pointed out one box: 'Bits of string no longer useful.' In addition to working on various aspects of the world ocean, Duchamp has made about six hundred maps of the Breton coast, both on shore and off shore. Talking about shores, he said if you looked closely at the pebbles on the shore at Trébeurden, only about a tenth of them are of local origin, all the others come from that very ancient river-complex of which what we now call the Rhine was the principal artery. Off shore, at isobath 140, you find a line of big stones, black-volcanic or granitic: the fishermen call them 'Carnac'. These are boulders that were swept down during the ice age by the currents from Scandinavia or western Scotland. You have to imagine a great lump of ice floating down the North Sea, landing on what was then the Breton shore, melting, and leaving the boulder it had at its heart . . . Duchamp knows the morphology of the Breton coast as a whole better than anybody, but, he says, there's always a fisherman acquainted with some little patch better than himself. He'd met up with one man who could sail over a meandering underwater gulch, taking his bearings from this or that landmark on shore. The man had great fishing over that gulch, but he'd never go there when there was any other boat in sight. It was only to Duchamp that he revealed the secret. My friend Jean-Paul has also taken thousands of underwater photographs: from some you see a fish staring out at you from the greyness. I came away from the study that first day with some panoceanic maps, but also with images of paleo-geographical rivers, ice-coated boulders borne on complex currents from Skye or from the Lofoten, and the eyes of fish gleaming in fathoms of darkness.

Finally there's the engraver Roland Chaunu, who lives at Tréduder, just back of Saint-Michel-en-Grève. Roland was born in Montargis, not far from Orléans. That was in the early 1930s. Then the war broke out and it was the exodus. He remembered travelling down the Loire first in a lorry then on a horse-cart, to the sound of machine-guns, his eye on a can of curds that stood under the seat. He was back up in Montargis in 1944 – they were gathering potatoes in the fields when the first American tanks arrived. A few years later, he was in the army at Algiers, as a radio operator. By 1956 he was in Paris, working in bookshops and drawing: mostly heads and torsoes whirling in baroque confusion. One of the bookshops he worked in was in the Rue du Bac, run by a Russian, Simonov, who also had a little publishing house, *Les Ponts de Paris*. It was a stormy household, the Simonovs'. One day a woman was haggling over a book: 'You could lower the price.' 'In front of ladies, I only lower my pants,' retorted the said Simonov with his usual finesse, at which his wife took off one of her shoes and shied it with slavic vigour at his head. Roland left to start up his own bookshop, in the Rue des Grands-Augustins, specialising in every branch of 'strange literature' (English gothic novels, science fiction, and so on). But he soon got tired of all the talk that went on in the shop: the same crowd would be there day after day discussing their heads off, building up piles of theoretical rhetoric about some trifle. That's when he decided to drop it all and come out to Brittany. He lived at first in a huge fifteenth-century manor, on which he spent a lot of time, trying to keep it from falling into ruin, then in a farm-house at Tréduder. In 1976, from a Dutchman who ran a small publishing house on a barge moored at the Quai de Conti in Paris, he bought a wooden press, a rare model dating from the early nineteenth century. That was when he began engraving in earnest. It was dry point to start with. The 'points' are normally of diamond, saphire or steel; Roland, out of necessity, the mother of invention, bought up dentist tools and worked them over. From there he moved to etching, working with iron perchloride and nitric acid. To his wooden press he came to add a metal one. And worked away like hell in his Breton solitude.

He showed me work he had ready and in progress: two frescoes of rocky landscape, and something that was part landscape, part musical score. Maybe some day we could do a big book together on the coast?

THE ARMORICAN YEAR

It was the carpenter, after finishing the shelves in the library late October, who came out with the significant phrase: 'So, you're going to be staying the winter?'

Obviously, he hadn't considered this possibility before. He'd taken it for granted that, like so many other old houses in the area, Gwenved was destined to be a summer residence. Now he saw that it was to be our permanent abode, it was as though he was saying: 'Ah, you're becoming one of us!'

There are in fact people in Paris who just can't understand how anyone would want to live, once the pleasant summer months are over, in such an out-of-the-way place as this. Isn't it cold and dark, they say, isn't it wild and wet and stormy? Isn't it lonely, even deadly, with no visitors, no cultural events? My dear people, you don't realise how much most 'cultural events' bore me, how much I just don't need them, and you are apparently unaware of the sheer delight in living a solitary and secluded life. You have lost touch with a whole dimension of existence. As for the cold and the dark, well, we're not exactly in the Polar Circle here: the climate is Armorican, that is to say oceanic, never *very* cold, and darkness falls later here in the west than in Paris.

But as from November, darkness does fall around six o'clock, and the days are often rainy. Which is why the months from November to February are called in Breton *ar miziou du* ('the dark months'). And there are some Bretons who say they don't like them either. 'November's a sad month,' said the dentist to me the other day in Lannion. I myself just can't feel things that way. It's not that I claim to be biologically or psychologically original. I wouldn't *want* to be biologically or psychologically original. But I positively delight in what is commonly called 'bad' weather. 'It's because you were born in Scotland', somebody will say. Maybe so, maybe so.

I take great pleasure in those blustery and rainy days of late November. Sometimes the wind will be tearing at the window all night, and then die away suddenly at seven in the morning, leaving a strange silence. Or else it will continue through the day, driving ragged cloud and blowing sheets of rain. I love walking along the deserted beach on those days, seeing the grey-white gulls scattering like shreds torn off the tide. I gaze with delight on the amazing colours of bramble leaves in December: green, black, orange, red. There are all kinds of things to hear and see that you don't see and hear in the summer. Those grey days in November and December (and sometimes into March and April) are never just grey. They're all shades of grey, and sometimes they're grey-blue, grey-mauve, grey-rose (like the pebbles of quartz and amethyst you can find at Pors Mabo). You can be walking along the path at Ploumanac'h, for example, with the whole seascape bathed in silvery grey, and suddenly a shaft of sunlight will illuminate one of the Seven Islands in smoky emerald green.

I've said that, the climate being atlantico-oceanic, the weather is never very cold here. But there can be exceptions to that. And the first winter we spent at Gwenved was exceptionally exceptional, with snow and icy winds.

Snow fell that year on Ushant for the first time in a century, and here in the Lannion Bay area we were actually blocked in for about two weeks.

It began quietly enough, with cold and rain and wind.

I remember one late October evening coming out of the Lannion municipal library, where I'd been consulting some old books, and meeting Yann Kervannec, the slater, on the steps leading down to the Rue Jean-Savidan:

'Awful weather', he said.

'I suppose so, but, really, I like it.'

'Me too, after all, now you say it. My father was a clog-maker. If you wanted to sell clogs, it had to rain. So whenever it rained, my father would say, great, we're going to sell some clogs.'

Early and mid-November were days and days of grey windy rain. Then towards the end of the month, we had some violent storms that shifted the layout of the beaches, carrying away dunes and flooding some towns.

By December, that chill keen wind known familiarly as the Moscow–Paris was blowing, making the telephone wires howl, the trees groan and scouring the sands.

Snow began to fall in January, but it soon let up, to begin again seriously in February. Sometimes it would be rainy snow hissing through the greyness, at other times salt-thin snow wisping and spiralling round the house. Then it would be a blizzard, the sea steel-grey and an apricot-coloured flush on the horizon. I'd watch the gulls and magpies making difficult headway through the salty-floury flurries, listen to a crow calling in the valley across a blurred red sunrise . . .

The snow fell thicker, thicker, thicker.

By mid-February, the area was a little Siberia – an impression reinforced by the presence of the nineteen birch trees we had planted in the garden. The Chemin du Gwaker, our little country road lined with hawthorn, was like the Tract, the old Russian postal track across the steppe. There were stalactites hanging from the gutters of the house, the library was sheathed in ice, and when the wind blew, the ice on trees, bushes and bamboo crackled and tinkled. It was beautiful and strange and very silent, with only that icy tinkling, or the occasional caw of a crow, or the yell of a gull, or the blethering of a goat.

The thaw came in March. I remember walking down the road to Pors Mabo, and seeing the toll those Siberian days had taken among the smaller birds. In one ditch, I found five little thrushes huddled together for warmth. It had really been a tough time, and very unusual in these parts. I have seen nothing like it since out here on the coast, and am told it's unlikely to happen again soon. But who knows?

Those winter months, I'll be in my studio just after daybreak. A lone gull will be crossing the red sky of the East. I'll hear the crow of a cock, the rush of the tide on Beg Leguer beach, and a tractor stuttering into action on a nearby farm . . .

I love to read old books, and consult old maps, with the rain swirling round the house. The other night, I picked out from the shelves Shakespeare's *Tempest*, and came across passages that were practically descriptions of the reality around me: 'An acre of barren ground – long heath, brown furze'; 'another storm brewing, I hear it sing in the wind'; 'being transported and rapt in secret studies'; 'all dedicated to closeness'; 'the isle is full of noises'; 'through forthrights and meanders'; 'the seamarge'; 'toothed briars, sharp furzes, pricking goss and thorns'; 'this is as strange a maze as e'er men trod' . . .

I'd like to apply to these winter months in Armorica, though maybe for different reasons, the name the Kwakiutl give winter on the north-west coast of America: 'the season of secrets.'

Here in Brittany, you may just be out of some heavy storm-weather at the end of January, and you'll already be seeing the first signs of spring, mimosa beginning to bloom. By the month of March, when the Laughing Gull returns to our coast, the *Crêperie des Îles* will be taking down its shutters in Trébeurden, the hotel *Ty al Lannec* overlooking the beach of Tresmeur will be welcoming its first guests, and then it will be those days nostalgically evoked by Chateaubriand, 'the days that precede the month of May and which our old poets of Gaul called Aprilean'.

I don't think I've ever experienced an Aprilness of such delicate subtlety as in Brittany. That the country should be half-way between north and south is part of it, that it should be open to the west, but not too open, is another.

Whatever the reasons, the result is strangely and quietly beautiful.

You see a band of gulls flying in a pale-blue sky. You know they're gulls, but all you actually see is a line of white flurries and flashes. Here and there, nestled in protected places, patches of primrose. The buttery-smelling bloom of the whin has been out for some time, and will be out a long time longer. The eye dwells lovingly on the circular rosy intricacy of the camelia. Starry blossoms have appeared on the acute-angled twigs of the blackthorn.

I've mentioned the gulls, but they're not alone. The walls of the house are noisy with sparrows. Blackbirds stab for worms in the dewy grass. A band of crows caw-caw darkly in the valley. A jay screeches and streaks off in a blue flash. Magpies swoop about on immaculate business. Two tits arrived yesterday, as well as a customer never seen before: a green-yellow fellow with a dark-red head . . .

April in Armorica!

I watch a waspy little creature hovering a foot above the earth, who'll suddenly zing off a yard or so and, then, just as suddenly, come back to his post. I don't exactly know what he's up to, but the mobility of it all delights me.

In the mornings, Pors Mabo beach is wrapped in blue mist. Heavy tides will have perhaps left a thick pile of jetsam: bits of dinghies, a box of clementines from Valencia . . . And another part of the cliff will maybe have subsided. You can read the cliff like a book laid open, with its geological chapters of clay and stone.

I usually go to one of my favourite rocks down there, and lie out, just listening to the tide.

The arrival of summer is marked at Gwenved by the taking out of the white metal table and chairs from the tool-shed and their setting up in the little 'monk's garden'. We'll be sitting out there, having a late lunch maybe (Catou, the cat, about whom more later, loves those lunches too), when we'll hear a band of hikers moving along the GR track from Lannion to Trébeurden.

Then there are the first voices on the beach.

Maybe it'll be an English father addressing his twelve-year-old daughter:

'Katie, you've done it again! You've gone an' put bloomin' sand on the marg!'

Or it will be typical Parisian street-talk like this:

'They say there are vipers in Brittany.'

'That's right. Tons of them.'

'When you drive over them, it doesn't kill them, they get up and keep running.'

'Right again. If you want to make sure you've got them, you've got to take them length ways.'

'Granma saw one the other day on the road. It had been run over but it was still moving.'

'Right. But you should have seen the face it made in the mirror!'

It's true that the Breton summer can be slow coming in – some people (and I can't pretend they're *entirely* wrong) will say there are years in which it doesn't come in at all . . . Early July, you can still be enmeshed, enshrouded in the greyness of Atlantic depressions, or in fog. Then, suddenly, one day, there it is, an oceanic blueness (caerulean, the painters call it), a zephyric wind, and a gentle warmth, as in an old Breton weather proverb I got from Roparz Gouessant: *Brumenn diwar ar mor, tommder en gor* ('Fog rising from the sea means heat'). That's when we begin regularly to have lunch out in the 'monk's garden', maybe with a little Anjou wine like a mixture of sunset and violets, or some dark, fruity, gravelly Bordeaux. At those times, you're totally at peace with the world.

One of the ideas we'd had in setting up house in Brittany was to be able to dispense with 'holidays'. If you live in a town, even a little town, it's understandable that you should want to spend at least a week or two a year in less congested space, and get your feet back naked on the ground. Hence the annual civilisational rush to the hills and the coasts – and more congestion. Our idea had been to integrate the 'holy days' into the normal run of things. Be able just to open the door and stroll barefoot round the garden, or walk down the valley, or along the coast.

Of course, that civilisational rush gets at you too now and then. The other day (I'm writing this in summer) a car with a rubber dinghy strapped to its roof stopped in front of the house and the slob at the wheel nonchalantly emptied his ashtray, obviously convinced that the world was his dustbin. A few lines back, I talked of people walking the coast. Ah, if only they did just that! But most spread themselves all over the place, leaving all kinds of trash: beer bottles, cigarette packets, and the rest. In summer, my sacred little shrine of the five pines off the coastal path turns into a shit-house, littered with bits of pink and white tissue paper. And then there are the guys who can't see a little path skirting the coast, going up and down, in and out, without thinking of Sport, in the shape of mountain-bikes. So that instead of coming up against a fellow walker on the coast, or, at most, a conscientious jogger, you encounter a black-and-crimson crash-helmeted zombie pedalling like a nitwit and raising a cloud of dust. Not to speak of those who can't see a cliff without thinking of gliding, or a stretch of water without thinking of windsurfing. And then there are the families whose only idea of pleasure is to make noise. I saw one the other day: mama, papa, young son, young daughter and baby. The son had a radio, the daughter had a Walkman, and the wean on the father's shoulders was already such a victim of civilisation that all it could do to express its happiness was to shout: 'Bang, bang, bang', while making a gesture of shooting up the universe.

But all this quietens down in September. That's when the lovely Grève Blanche comes back into its own. In the immense stillness, only the sounds of seabirds: *ke-kwek-kwek, tee-wee-la-o* . . . In the shallow water, a shoal of little blue eel-like fishlets. Glistening spider-webs on the rocks of Île-aux-Lapins. The sun will leave a coppery path on the pale grey of the sea, and then about midday the mist will come ghosting up and the whole coast will be wrapped in it all afternoon.

I had been told there were foxes in the valley of Goaslagorn, but I'd never seen any. I'd seen foxgloves, plenty of them, but never a fox. Then one October evening . . .

I was walking along the little path through the valley down to the seacoast, minding my own business, enjoying the sunlit breeze, when suddenly I was aware of an animal on the path, about a dozen yards ahead of me, also minding its own business, and also enjoying the sunlit breeze. I admit that my first thought was: that's a very big, very strange-looking cat – and then it was suddenly obvious: no, you idiot, it's not a cat, it's a fox! No sooner had that thought crossed my mind than the fox flashed off, turning down a path to the left. I followed up quietly, went down that winding path to the left a few steps myself, without much hope – and had just time to see the fox's tail disappear into a clump of fern.

I stood still for a while, just in case he came out again, but he didn't, so I went back up the little winding path and continued on my way.

But I felt privileged at even seeing Fox. I felt as if I'd been let into the secret life of the country. And from that moment on, I've continued to see him now and then: running, red, over the brown earth of a ploughed field, hunched under a pine tree, or slinking along the path of Pors Mabo.

An Atlantic Studio

My workroom is laid out on a west-east axis, so that I go to work with the rising sun in one window, and finish it with the setting sun in the other.

On the ledge of the east-facing window are inscribed two phrases. One is from a Western poet, Sophocles: *pantoporos aporos* ('having wandered everywhere, now nowhere'). The other consists of three Chinese ideograms: two wings and a whiteness, the sun caught in the branches of a tree, and then sun and moon together, the whole meaning 'to persevere in the morning light'.

On the ledge of the western window that faces the sea lie binoculars and a collection of bird books.

The library is downstairs. At work, I prefer to have all the books, or at least the great majority of them, below me, rather than around me.

When the removers delivered the boxes of books to Gwenved, they told me there were three tons of them. That was ten years ago. There must be at least five tons now.

At first, with shelves running round three walls, I thought I had plenty of room. But I pretty soon had books in double rows practically everywhere. Until, within the library, I had a little alcove built, which gave me two more walls. I'd been a bit afraid that extra construction would eat up the nice sensation of space I had down there, but in fact, no, it's just complexified things a bit.

The manuscripts, usually encased in coloured folders, lie on low shelves running round the room, or else on the floor. When they're on the floor, the piles are topped by a stone. That's because I like the look of those stones, which come from various parts of the globe, but it's also for practical reasons. The Armorican promontory is windy, and if you open the door on some days, without the stones, the sheets would be flying all over the place.

Talking about winds, there's a book I'd like to have, here in my Atlantic library: Henry Piddington's *Conversations about Hurricanes*, published in London, in the middle of the nineteenth century. Henry Piddington was curator of the Museum of Economic Geology in Calcutta. It was after a ship he commanded had been dismasted by a storm and only saved by a lull that he turned his attention to meteorology. He it was who invented the word 'cyclone'.

There are no cyclones in this area, I'm happy to say, though we sometimes get the tail ends of them. But there are big winds enough and plenty of storms.

The prevailing wind here of course is the west wind, the sea-wind, warmish and wet. But we also get a taste of winds from the Arctic, coming down via Iceland and Scotland, winds that are *cold*. And those winds sometimes meet, together with the south-west tropical winds coming up over the Gulf of Gascony. All that makes for interesting weather and a very variable sky.

I like to know I have all that weather at my window. I rejoice to hear the hail storms of March blustering in from the west in a sub-Arctic dance. I enjoy watching white gobs and streaks of sleet running down the panes. But it's especially the wind, a constant companion, snuffling or whooming. 'Well before the Flood there was a powerful creature, without flesh and without bones', says a poem of the Welshman Llywarch Hen. I like that, but I like even more, for its sheer austerity and the absence in it of fantasm and mythology, that line from a Gaelic poem out of the Annals of Tigernach: 'The wind is cold on Islay.'

As I said, there are two windows: the land-window and the sea-window. Beneath the first, a field of sturdy maize, across the other, a field of silky rye. From them, I followed all one night a constellation in the sky, wanting also to see how fast the moon travelled. If in general I like to have my feet on the ground, I don't mind an odd outing among the meteors. In the Syriac apocalypse of Baruch, Baruch visits five skies, and learns worlds about the sun, the moon, the stars, the wind and the rain.

There's a photograph of Montaigne's tower on one wall of my workroom. There are also photographs of Nietzsche's inn at Sils Maria, Thoreau's hut at Walden, an engraving of Spinoza's workshop at Rhynnsburg, a Chinese geomantic diagram of a hermitage in the hills . . .

There are several maps too: of Labrador and Newfoundland, China and Japan, the Pacific islands, the forest areas of America, the geology of the Armorican peninsula, and the five square kilometres around the house . . .

Then there are images of birds, mammals and fishes: the American pelican, the snowy owl, the grey heron, the gannet, the kingfisher, seals, whales, bears, wolves . . .

There are also phrases and fragments of poems, reproductions of Japanese prints ('Sunset on a snowy day at Uchikawa', 'Kambara, snow at night'), alphabets, lists, diagrams . . .

Down in the library, there's a Japanese compass, an Aïnu totem, an Amerindian mask, more maps, and a big chunk of blue coral . . .

All this creates the context in which I feel at home, in which I like to work.

A poem by Marban the hermit says it all very well:

> *Fair birds come here*
> *gulls and herons*
> *the sea singing*
> *no mournful music*
> *brown grouse*
> *rising from red heather*
>
> *Sounds of wind*
> *in the branchy wood*
> *grey cloud and waterfalls*
> *the cry of a swan*
> *delightful music*

I work in here about twelve hours a day. Around eight in the morning, I'll be crossing the yard with a pot of tea (a heavy black cast-iron Japanese teapot) and one of the bowls made by my friend the potter. Let's say it's a winter morning, overcast, no stars to be seen, only a light in the neighbouring farm, a misty light from behind trees, and, down to the south-west there, the noise of the waves on the beaches of Lannion Bay. I switch on the lamp and the heater, sit at my table, pour myself a bowl of tea, and the day's work begins . . .

When I say 'work', that doesn't mean always writing, or reading. It can mean just sitting, looking round the room, or taking the binoculars to look at some bird through the window, or walking round the garden, or just contemplating the slow dance of the clouds.

This is my hermitage, my cosmopoetic laboratory, my intellectual lighthouse.

In Old English (West Saxon), there's a word *anhaga*, 'one who lives alone'. That *haga* is maybe connected with 'hedge' and means enclosure, dwelling. Another word close to this one is *anhoga*, from *hogian*, to think. If you bring them both together, you get something like: 'one who meditates in solitude'.

'To be a poet-scholar requires a lot of silence,' says an old Chinese poem.

Atlantic atopia.

I think often in here of Sinlanus, known as *famosus mundi magister* (famed teacher of the world), who taught in the monastic school of Bangor and who wrote the earliest Irish chronicle. I think of Milton's *Penseroso*: 'Our happiness may orb itself into a thousand vagrancies of glory and delight and with a kind of eccentrical equation be, as it were, an invariable planet of joy and felicity' – conscious of the sheer delight to be obtained from learning and thinking, the absolute *contentation* (an old Elizabethan word) of it all. I think of Fenollosa's remarks on Michael Angelo, in his *Epochs of Chinese and Japanese Art*: 'Michael Angelo, holding back, single-handed, like a grand promontory half-submerged by storms, the mediocrity due to a flippant and corrupt *cinquecento*.' I think of Yuan Hong-da, speaking about his book on clouds and stones: 'This is not for vulgar literary people. It is a joy to be savoured by fervent travellers and contemplative hermits.' I think of Josep Brodski, in his *Letter to a Roman Friend*: 'If one is forced to be born in Caesar's empire, let him live aloof, provincial, by the seashore.'

This is my Patmos.

Where else can an intellectual nomad take up residence but in a Patmos?

This is my hyperborean Patmos . . .

Though my intention here has never been to write an Apocalypse. Maybe something like the old Celtic text *The Black Book of Carmarthen*. Let's say a 'Red book of Trébeurden'.

It's when the mist is thick around my lonely stony house, like this morning, that I really have the impression of living in some old monastery of the times when the cranes were still dancing among the reeds of the Shannon. And the impression is even stronger when, like this morning again, I'm copying out manuscripts, as in some ancient scriptorium.

I've always copied out texts, with the idea that by so doing I could sort of *incorporate* them. Down in the library, I've got copies of Rimbaud's *Saison en enfer*, say, or Wallace Stevens' *The Man with the Blue Guitar* done in rented rooms in foggy Glasgow or in my attic room in Fairlie with Arran of the stags on the horizon and gulls yelling ecstatically over the skylight.

But these were done on ordinary paper with the instrument that was to hand: an ordinary pen using ordinary ink.

For the last few years, however, there's been an extension of this practice that goes beyond mere copying. Painter-friends will supply me with books (in several copies, usually three or four) made from all kinds of paper which they have coloured with watercolour and gouache. I live with them for a while, thinking out a suitable text, then write it.

At the moment, I have three copies of a biggish volume, 12" by 6", bound in tarry black with a red blaze on the cover and, inside, thick sheets coloured in various ways: with sepia washes, with strokes of blue and red, with semaphore flashes, precipitous rushes, stretches of clear emptiness and sharp breaks. Those painters know the kind of background, the kind of atmosphere, the kind of rhythm I like.

So I clear the writing table, bring out the scallop shell in which I pour the thick black heavy Chinese ink, and choose my pen. I've written with all kinds of instruments: with a sharpened bamboo, with a twig from a hawthorn tree; with graphoplex technical pens of varying sizes, but at the moment I'm using an ordinary pen-holder with a special nib I was able to acquire recently in Paris, at a little shop just down from the Pantheon.

In Alexandria, they used to write on papyrus. Then, when Eumenes, in Pergamon, wanting to set up a big library, had to face the Egyptian papyrus monopoly, he was obliged to find a new basis. This he did, and it was parchment: animal skin starched and stretched. Paper we've been using only since the thirteenth century, thanks to the Chinese, via the Arabs and Spain.

Let's look in on a medieval scriptorium.

The writer has his parchment ready, and he's sharpened his goose quill, and his ink is in his ox-horn. The basis for this ink might be sloe-bushes. They'd gather twigs in April or May, let them lie a couple of days, then hammer off the bark and leave them steeping in water for another two or three days more. That gave a reddish-brownish liquid that was then cooked, with the bark, and at the end wine was added: the mixture was dried in the sun (you diluted with more wine for later use). You could get nuances of colour by adding, for example, a glowing piece of iron. You could get red tints by using cinnabar, and other tints with other minerals or plants or shellfish: malachite giving mountain green; lapislazuli, ultramarine blue; murex, purple; crocus, safran yellow . . .

Maybe it's Ireland or Iona, about the sixth century. Think of Saint Columba's *Cathach*, or the Book of Durrow, the Book of Armagh, the Book of Kells, the Book of the Dun Cow (*Lebor na Huidre*), Celtic influences combining with Syrian and Coptic to give something strangely original. Columba, Colum of the churches (Colum-Cille), is said himself to have copied out three hundred manuscripts in his own hand.

I move from Iona to Japan, thinking of the twelfth-century collection of poems by the 'thirty-six poetic geniuses' written on Tsugigami paper, or again the sutra donated to the Itsukushima

Shrine by the Tira Clan, written out on a background of leaves and waves, or Fujiwara Korefusa's manuscript of the *Genji Monogatari*, written on a ground of browny gold like some splendid autumn.

A December day, thick mist round the house. Dipping my pen regularly in the scalloped ink, and writing out the book. Big silence, only the pen scraping, and the book growing page after page after page.

Where are we?

In a poetic paradise.

A morning in eternity.

A Bibliophile Fantasia

I f my Atlantic library is pretty well stocked with books (a few thousand volumes in several languages) and in maps (all kinds of atlases, portulans and charts), it also has a special section devoted to manuscripts. I don't mean my own manuscripts, I'm referring to old texts I've managed to sniff out and pick up here and there since I took up residence in these Armorican parts.

I am, for example, the glad possessor of Brother Kenec's manuscript. It's one of the first I was able to get my hands on, inaugurating with it my collection.

Written in the cursive hand which was habitually used in France, Germany, Switzerland, Flanders and Italy in the fifteenth century, and which is usually referred to as *Oberrheinische Bastarda*, this manuscript (parchment and paper) of 231 pages, bound in leather, was composed in Brittany, at Guingamp, about 1425, by a man who calls himself, at the end of the text, Frère Kenec.

All we know about Brother Kenec is that he had been a student at Poitiers and that he travelled a good deal in Germany, in Switzerland (he speaks with nostalgia of Basel) and in Italy, where he lived at Sienna and at Venice.

He talks very little about himself, but the manuscript speaks for him.

Brother Kenec's manuscript opens with a map of the Atlantic showing clearly the Isle of St Brandan, the Isle of Antilia and a stretch of coast called Vinlandia. After the map comes *The Peregrination of St Brandan*, an extract from the *Speculum maius* by Vincent de Beauvais, a few poems, some of which have been translated into Latin from Breton and Gaelic, others being no doubt by Kenec himself. The manuscript comes to a close with a very strange, fragmentary text entitled *Speculum cosmopoeticum*.

Another of my *opuscula armoricana* is the manuscript of Conrad O'Connor, which I found away in a musty corner of a second-hand bookshop in St Malo.

Conrad O'Connor was a doctor, a whaler and a rough-diamond kind of poet.

Born in Greenock, on the west coast of Scotland, about 1842, O'Connor pursued medical studies at Glasgow. By 1870, he was ship's doctor aboard the *Northern Lights* of Peterhead, Captain Andrew Melville. Ten years later, we find him at St Malo, aboard *L'Intrépide*, Captain Joseph Michaux. He retired from the service about 1898, in the Azores, living in a little house at the edge of a *misterioso*, the name given in the islands to the lava landscapes that lie at the foot of the volcano.

At a certain point in his career, in France, O'Connor was commissioned to write reports on sailors' living conditions and on fishing techniques round the world. It's those reports, written in French, that constitute the bulk of his papers.

But there are also descriptions of islands and ports (Madagascar, Montevideo, New Bedford . . .) and a sheaf of long poems, written in English, mostly unfinished.

Towards the end of his life, O'Connor was much addicted to the local wine of the Azores, the *venho verdelho*. But his favourite potion, as his journals show, was *kawa*, that non-alcoholic, non-intoxicating beverage of the Navigator Isles, which stimulates dreams.

It was at the bottom of a trunk, in the loft of an old house in Lannion, that I found the following text, written in Breton. Its date is uncertain, its source also. I've entitled it *The Surveyor*:

'He came to live in our neighbourhood one year, about the turn of the century, at the beginning of winter. I was twelve years old at the time. We were never very sure what his profession was: artist, surveyor, or whatever. When people asked him what he was doing in these parts, he'd invariably answer: "I've come to see." To see what? Nobody really had any idea. We'd see him on the moors and on the narrow paths round the coast, in all weathers, but especially in the kind of weather or at the time of day when nobody else would be about: rainy days, or dawns. I know he read a lot, or at least that he had read a lot at one time. One day, at his place, I saw what he called his "workshop". It was full of books in many different languages. Some, that had been set aside, bore a word in their titles: *mandala*. I looked it up in a dictionary, then in the encyclopedia: "A model of the universe (sanskrit: circle)", but at the time I didn't feel any further forward. Maybe, if he'd put those books aside, it was because he was no longer interested in models? Who could say? The man I called "the surveyor" didn't talk much himself. I remember one day, again at his place, I saw a sheet of paper bearing these words: "And one

evening we arrived in the maritime provinces, lands that smell of
seaweed and salt, and that are bathed in storm-light." But he had
crossed them out and in the margin he'd printed just one word in big
letters: "OVERDONE". I said he'd read a lot. I remember the titles of
other books I saw. They intrigued me, and I noted them down,
because I was beginning to be interested in books myself: *The Lessons of
Sinlan, La Rivière inconnue, Historia de controversiis quas Pelagius eiusque
reliquiae moverunt, Meer und Wüste* . . . I don't think he could be called
'a writer', at least not in the usual sense. He wrote, certainly, but
never anything but fragments on unconnected bits of paper. I'd seen
some of them: "Nothing happens, nothing happens – then there's the
leap"; "Keep a space open where the wild signs can come breaking
in"; "The field of insight is not the domain of knowledge"; "Living
outside the systems and the beliefs"; "One is closer to Being in being
nothing than in believing one is something." A philosopher? Perhaps.
But other bits of paper only carried lists, with no thought at all:
"Granite, sandstone, schist, quartz", "lapwing, skua, chough"; or else
little notes such as these: "All afternoon, at the foot of the apple-tree,
in the mist"; "the October moon on Pors Mabo"; "the cold gold of
the grasses"; "a fire of salty wood in the hearth"; "full moon, Atlantic
rain"; "the workshop lit up red in the rising sun"; "a day the colour of
oysters"; "a few steps on the blue granite" . . . Others seemed to be
of a different category again: "meteorology of the mind"; "the
flotsam and jetsam of arguments scattered on the shore". When
he was outside, he'd have a kind of rucksack on his back in which he
carried paper and pencils for drawing. Hard to say exactly what he
drew: all I could see were lines and a multiplicity of touches here and
there – nothing that looked like anything, nothing that seemed to
have any coherence, and yet, curiously enough, I was attracted to it.
Maybe that's what he called "adventuring in the multiverse". I realise
that this portrait of him that I've undertaken to do is as incoherent as
his own drawings. This man was an enigma, and he remained so. He
left us, just as suddenly as he had come, one morning, leaving me

some books, his notes and his drawings, and this little note: "Maybe one day you too will want to *see*."'

I discovered the following text, written in Latin, in an old monastery on the coast, copied it out, and translated it under the title *The Unknown Territories*:

'At that time, I was living on the Promontory of the Winds, in wild Galloway, near the famous "white house" (*candida casa*) founded by Ninian. Those were the last days of the Roman empire in Brittania. The legions – those that remained (I'm thinking of the ninth Hispana, completely wiped out by the tribes) – were pulling out one after the other. The Batavians and all the rest of the mercenaries were trekking back to their homes. We felt a bit lonely, as though orphaned. There was fear and even panic in the air. The villa owners were burying their treasures in the fields, with an anxious eye to the northern frontier. Nobody had any faith any more in the walls raised by Hadrian and Antonine. Nobody had faith in anything. Except, maybe, some, in God. Ninian, for example. He was preparing an expedition, I mean a mission, to the tribes of the north-east which the Romans, never very precise about ethnographic detail ("a barbarian is a barbarian") had called *Picti*, that is, "the Pintos".

As for me (never mind my name), I have never believed in anything. Born in Aquitania, next door to a tribe called the *Pictones* (would they be cousins to those Picts of the north – who can tell?), I spent some time in Armorica before crossing the Celtic Sea. I lived for a while at Lugdunum, then at Luguvallium and at Castrum Exploratorum. I joined the auxiliaries, as a kind of observer, drawing up maps and charts. But for what really interested me, there was no name. Always curious about unknown lands, I was attracted to the North. It was at Castrum Exploratorum that I heard of Ninian, and decided to try and join his mission.

It was very hard to get a clear idea about the state of the tribes in the north. As an adolescent, I had read the life of Agricola (one-time governor of Aquitania) by Tacitus, and already at that time I was fascinated by the image of those northern shores. As well as by the glimpses one got here and there of the tribes: the Brigantes, the Borestri, the Silures, the Ordovices, the Votadini and the savage Attacotti – all those who lived "beyond the isthmus", in a "formless land". At Castrum Exploratorum, weird stories went the rounds: that those people lived in caves and were cannibals; that they ate only nuts and berries; that their houses were either made of tree trunks covered with slabs of peat and birch bark, or were nothing but reed and mud cabins set up in the middle of marshes . . . I wanted to see Caledonia and its inhabitants. I wanted to visit places such as Bodotria, Clota, Graupius Mons, Mona, Tanaus, Portus Trucculensis and those islands called the Orcades.

Armed with a stylet and a few tablets, I left in the company of Ninian the Culdee ("God's servant"), who had studied at Rome and in Gaul with Martin, the man who brought oriental ideas into the schools of the West. We set out for the north-east. To enter the unknown territories, there were two tracks: the one to the west, that went by Cathures, then a long lake, and followed the mountain chain of Drumalban; and the one to the east that went by Cramond, the isthmus and the wild rock of Dunnotar. Our path lay by Cathures, the highland country, the central plain, before coming to a very strange country with mountains rising to the sky like red islands in a desert. At every preaching stop, Ninian would chisel a cross on a stone, so as to mark and sanctify the place. And then he'd talk: about life and death, about the power of God. A great organiser too, he would found cells and churches – oh, very rough little churches, but churches all the same. As for me, I just kept on taking my sightings and drawing my contour maps, attracted less by Ninian's crosses than by the stones themselves, and, saying to myself, with an eye to the horizon, that it wasn't life and death that interested me, but the shapes of things. Less sanctification symbols than *penetration lines*.

The farther we went, the more frequent the Pictish signs became.

They were engraved on stones and on posts: geometric forms, with birds and animals, sometimes also a kind of writing: a vertical line and, on either side of it, groups of two, three or four strokes. Territorial marks, said some; magic, said others. I had no opinion. My only concern was to go farther on. In this Alba, I had the feeling, step after step, sign after sign, that I was making contact with some archaic dawn, obtaining access to arcane archives. One day, a Pict I met in the mountains took a piece of wood and with his knife cut a line on it. To the left of it, he then cut one stroke, then four strokes, then two strokes. *"Ogam"*, he said, and *"Bel"*. Of course I didn't understand a word. But I can say this: the Roman empire was time, well measured, rhythmic time; Christianity was time too, beginning with the birth of Christ, dated, always referred to; but here, I had a sensation of being outside time, moving through signs in space, entering a completely different area of culture.

It was obvious that those "Pintos" (they do in fact paint their bodies) had the souls of artists. You only had to look at their bronze brooches, their necklets of silver, their many-coloured cloth, their objects made of bone, stone, wood and amber. Yes, those Caledonians, creatures of shadow and dawnlight, fascinated me. But I was even more fascinated by the territories we crossed: great stretches of desert, forests of pine and birch, bird cries on the marshes, lakes of changing lights, bears, wolves, boars, otter, deer . . .

Ninian died in 432. I kept on wandering in the territories. I sailed along the coast in a Pictish boat (if they're great horsemen, they're also daring navigators), and have settled finally in a region that not even the tribes of the mist inhabit. I have a cell made of stone and wood at the edge of the forest. All around me, mountains, plateaux, cliffs: abrupt lines, trails of pebbles . . . It's a long time since I saw a regular writing or drawing tablet. But I still have my stylet. For a while I scraped lines on the rocks. Then I gave up even that. The earth has done it all so much better than me.

Sometimes, at night, in my cell, I look back on the past. I see a villa in Aquitania. I see a boat in an Armorican harbour. I see a windy promontory and a white house. I say to myself: you've known Aquitania, Armorica, Brittania, Alba . . . You've known catastrophes and cataclysms. Now here you are on the edge, at the limits, a man of nothing, a citizen of emptiness, a pilgrim of the void.'

So, there are my manuscripts.

Alter egos. Previous existences?

At the present moment I'm preparing a critical edition of Brother Kenec's manuscript that is likely to alter radically our conception of the Middle Ages. As for the papers of Conrad O'Connor, I intend to publish them in totality under the title *Kawa*. And with *The Surveyor* and *The Unknown Territories*, I think I'll make a couple of artist's books with my friend the engraver who lives in Tréduder.

The Paths of Stone and Wind

These last few days, cold rain-bearing winds have been sweeping over the north coast of Brittany and rough seas with gurly grey-green waves have been lunging in over the shores, sometimes changing local topographies: what was once bare sand in that north-eastern corner has turned into a chuckie field, and where before there was a mass of pebbles now there is only sifted sand and a line of wrack.

No doubt about it, the earth is an interesting place . . .

It's in wild weather like the one I've just evoked that I like to go out walking. Why? Well, because it gives you a strong sense of the elements, and then, you're practically sure of being on your lonesome. After a walk of a few miles, I like to sit in the lee of some rock, all around the wind howling and the rain drifting, with for company maybe only a little shred of red seaweed, or a bit of quartz whose tip is amethyst, or nothing at all.

For some people, activity, non-activity, such as this, is not only anti-social, it's inhuman. They would have us talking all the time about our father's old slippers or the problems of our daughter's children's children. I don't think the attraction to lonely space, elemental conditions and basic stone is inhuman, I think it's of the essence of human being on earth.

There's something like a ground-tone, spoken, played or graphed, that you can hear all round the earth. When once you've got on to its wavelength, a lot of what is called 'culture' shows up as inconsequential if not futile, and sounds hollow. But maybe every real culture is founded on that ground-tone, and on a fundamental dimension that carries an austere joyance.

This morning I went out to a secluded bay I know. I took my time walking round it, making for a small, raised stone half-hidden in the bracken. I spent a couple of hours with my back against it, doing little more than look into the rain.

It's probably to rock chaoses and to lone stones that my preference goes. But the man-made alignments and the circles also have their fascination.

Three agglomerations come immediately to the fore of my mind: Carnac in Brittany, Stonehenge in England, Callanish in Scotland. Stonehenge is the most massive. Carnac astounds by its sheer numbers. What gives Callanish, way up there in the outer Hebrides, its peculiar quality, is its savage solitude, as well as what I always feel as a certain grotesquerie in the shape of the stones and in their disposition, including, nowadays, the gaps.

I like to think of those raised stones as 'the Atlantic stones'. They've marked the Atlantic coastline for millennia and I've followed their megalithic cartography all the way from Portugal up to the Scottish archipelagoes. But I know they go farther back than the Atlantic. The Atlantic is what they face, but their background is maybe Anatolia. Out from Anatolia or thereabouts, the migration went to those lands later, much later, known as Italy, Sicily, Sardinia, Corsica, Spain, France, the Armorican peninsula (where there seems to be a peculiar concentration), England, Ireland, Scotland, Denmark, Sweden, Finland . . . The big stone road.

Imagine great monotonous stretches of uncharted, unnamed territory, imagine vast eroded plateau and postglacial beaches. The time is the end of the Boreal period, the beginning of the archaic times called 'Atlantic'. Sudden mists, strange lights and lightnings, and up there, far above, moon, sun, stars: appearances, disappearances, constellations. The earthscape is mineral, dominated by great stone blocks fallen from obscure disasters, and by scatterings of fragmented rock. In such a context, geometry (a point, a line, a circle) can be a kind of salvation, especially if you can feel that you're establishing a correspondence with what you haven't yet got round to calling a cosmos.

It's a world of primitive geometry and primal meteorology.

Later on, the stories come in. Some of these stories (you hear of petrified armies, of druid sacrifices, all kinds of spookiness and collective unconscious hookery-pookery) are more attractive than others. I like the Hebridean one that tells of craggy rocks arriving by boat on Lewis accompanied by folk (they sound like shamans) dressed in feathers . . . All this is what some people call 'poetry'. But the real poetics are elsewhere: in the open space, in the migratory movement, the elementary necessity, the primal gesture. You can go further by trying to read beyond the legends. Beginning with the grainy touch of the stone itself, and its lichens.

As to the theories, the interpretations and the calculations, I listen to them attentively, in a stony silence, before moving back to some rock, any old rock on shore or moor on which frost and sea-salt have written the weather of the ages.

If we had opted for a house in Brittany, in a relatively out-of-the-way place (though near enough to a post-office and a station – I'm a hermit with timetables at my elbow), it was also with the idea of just opening the door and, without an intermediary of any kind (car, bus or whatever), being able to start walking in any direction, sure of a beautiful, uncongested landscape.

This north coast of the Armorican peninsula has all those qualities.

The Trégor, our particular area, is a plateau cut by deep valleys and gullies running down to the sea. Because of Atlantic forces, its coast is ragged, fractured, extremely various. And it is rich in paths. Some of these go back to prehistory; these are the ones worn into the granite. Others are more recent, though not of fresh date, let's say eighteenth century. They go back to the times when smuggling was rife between here, the Channel Islands and the coast of England, with keg after keg of Cousin Jack, as the English called cognac, being shipped out on dark nights. The smuggling traffic meant vigilant patrol by the custodians of the law, hence the name of those tracks that skirt the headlands, giving a good view of the bays and coves: the *chemins des douaniers* ('excisemen's paths').

The two kinds of path I've just evoked, the archaic ones and the erstwhile excise paths, both come under the generic term in Breton *henchou koz*, the 'old paths'. Nowadays, except for a short visitors' season in summer, and apart from a very few, they're practically unfrequented. But in the days of yore, there would be all kinds of folk on them – charcoal-sellers, slaters, ragmen and strolling actors like this one, speaking in a peasants' mystery play:

> *A'll tell ye abat all the places A've bin*
> *Tho' none the wiser I am since first A set out*
> *A've my bite and my kip at Kerlomi town*

And at Plouenez A'm known without any a doubt
At Lanmoder A've bin and at Trogairi
At Pouldoman and at Miniby
A've tramped over to Paimpol, Plouez as well
And of Camlez parish A've heard the bell
Ma feet are familiar with the paths of Hengoat
The roads of La Roche, and the streets of Langouat . . .

I like to think of these folk now and then, when I walk the old paths, but most of the time I'm glad they're empty – empty of humanity, that is, because of course they're full of all sorts of other things.

If I want a short walk, and that's almost every day, I'll make for Pors Mabo.

In winter, I'll leave the house about half past four, in summer as late as seven or eight. First, I cross the Chemin du Gwaker, and take the path leading down into the valley of Goaslagorn, seeing the little chapel of St Tugdual there to my left. Thereafter I follow the path along the valley, passing by, with a little word or two of salutation, Loïc Rannou's pink pigs and tawny-hided goats, till I come to the crest of the hill overlooking Lannion Bay. I usually stop there a while for the view, then go down the stony way among the red campions and the wild rose bushes till I get on to the exciseman's path that runs along the little cliff to the north-west. In winter the steady light from Dourven Point will be already on, and away over towards Roscoff I'll see another lighthouse blinking on and off, with a flash of four seconds (three times), then an interval of twelve. My next stop will be at the Grove of the Five Pines, a little dark-red, dark-green space among the whin and fern, where I'll sit with my back to one of the tree-trunks facing the setting sun, and maybe a blackbird on a branch beside me, unaware of my presence, or at least not worried by it. I continue on among the pines, then it's moorland and a crag, with maybe a crow cawing on it, and gulls yelling over the water, and perhaps a heron, greyblue and silent, on a sea-rock. When I get to Parc ar C'han, I follow an even smaller little path, lined by long trailers of bramble and cross two wooden bridges, till I reach the beach. Say it's a December evening, about five o'clock, the sea oystergreen. To the west, towards the land's end, in the grey of the gloaming, a smattering of red. In the gathering darkness of the bay, the plaintive call of a sound-buoy, and the steady light over by Locquémeau, leaving no trace on the waters, but at the tide's edge, a great golden exclamation mark.

I've just evoked the 'Grove of the Five Pines'. I wouldn't like to pinpoint it too exactly on the map (I'll be forgiven, I hope, this little secret), but it's a place we should linger at a while, at least in spirit.

For me, it's a place of musical meditation.

There's a music of the landscape. It has rarely been listened to. Maybe before civilisation, but even then. Maybe primitive man really listened only to the sounds liable to have an immediate effect on his life, his survival: the cracking of a branch signalling the approach of an animal, the rising of the wind announcing a tempest . . . Far from entering into the great relationship, he was only interested in what related to himself. But it could be I'm exaggerating. Maybe, here and there, there were ears able to listen in to the pure music of the landscape that announces nothing. What is certain is that with the arrival of civilisation, and especially its development, people stopped listening in to anything like this. They listened to political harangues, to religious homelies, to all kinds of fabricated music, and to themselves. It's only now (the end of a civilisation?) that, in isolated places, individuals have begun again to *listen to the landscape*.

Sometimes you can get the feeling that it's too late. Maybe this is the age of the last landscapes. The trees do not bear themselves so well as before. The sea is sick to the teeth of swallowing refuse and offal. Some of us who listen sometimes get the impression that they're hearing subdued complaints, murmurs of agony. Maybe it's just our own conscience projecting its voice. But that conscience is also part of the world. And if it is bad, the reception of the music of the world will be bad too. Hence that interference, that stridence.

I still keep trying to listen in . . .

Friends tell me I should practise what they call *zazen*, 'sitting meditation'. This is a practice they have borrowed from a Far-Eastern tradition for which I have the greatest respect. So they gather together in a hall, usually in town, or in big country residences, they take up the appropriate posture, and they meditate. Fine, I approve without reservation. It does them a lot of good, they're less nervous. They even approach a calm kind of wisdom. And I don't despise wisdom, that archaic notion, I don't make fun of it, not at all. It's just that, well, I want my wisdom to be in touch with things and to keep all its senses open. I don't want a kind of somnambulistic wisdom, a wisdom without breaks.

So I go on with my own little practices. I sit with my back to a pine, I look at the setting sun, and I listen – to the murmur of the sea, to the sound of the wind in the pine branches. No doubt I listen in also to my conscience, that in me which knows, which thinks, and which sometimes would like to obliterate itself. But I go on, I go on listening, until I hear something. What? It's not hope I hear (I'd be ashamed of that); it's not a song, a chant, a hymn, a psalm; it's next to nothing. And it doesn't last. But it's all I need. That gives me the basis on which I can go on existing and working, in my own way. After that little exercise, I get up, and it's now my habits really become ridiculous. I go slowly from one tree-trunk in the grove to another. I put my two hands on the rough bark, and leave them there awhile (to measure the 'while' I use a pretty complex method of counting). When I've gone the rounds, and I've come back to the first tree, I put my two arms around it, then I leave.

You see now why I didn't want to be too precise about the location of my Grove of the Five Pines. It's not so much that I fear crowds, but maybe just now and then somebody vaguely curious. My practice is so idiosyncratic it should be witnessed by no one. Just imagine if the curious visitor was a psychiatrist. They'd shut me up. They'd invent a name for my case. Whereas all I am, when you get down to it, is half the ghost of an old shaman and half the offspring of a pythagorician.

I like to stand at the custom's lookout post above the estuary of the Léguer, up at Coz Yaudet. You see the ribs of a wrecked boat on the mudflats, and if you look down over the rivermouth, it's to contemplate a green sea swirling round the coppergreen beacons. You can see Locquémeau, the spot where the *Azalea* was wrecked off Dourven, and imagine the whole spit of land that sweeps round Lannion Bay up to Morlaix and Roscoff, much frequented in bygone days by Captain Harry Carter, the smuggler from Cornwall.

I'm often on the path too that lies between Locquémeau and Saint-Michel-en-Grève.

Locquémeau, the 'hermitage of St Kemo', is a quiet little fishing village on the opposite bank of the Léguer from Trébeurden. There is the *bourg*, snuggled round its old church, and the harbour, with its road laid over a stony causeway. Down at the pier, you find a shed where the fishing smacks store their lobster creels and other paraphernalia, a restaurant and a curiosity shop.

The exciseman's path starts from a spot situated just before the place where the road from the village turns into the road to the harbour. Say it's a grey day, with the sun lighting up patches of emerald in a dark-green sea. Maybe the first things you'll notice are the pink flowers of the bramble, but there are all kinds of growths along the path from Locquémeau to St-Michel: ferns and thorns in abundance, with heather, gorse and whin. Also, now and then, pine trees. And even bamboo, no doubt the remains of some cultivated garden that has scattered and gone wild. You walk high above black basaltic rocks, or grey-green rocks covered with red-yellow lichen or very black lichen, beautiful to see, especially with the green sea pounding against them in white foam. Now and then you'll come across a cormorant on some rock drying its wings.

When the wind blows really strong, and when there's a storm brewing, I like to walk round the path of Île-Grande. Yes, for walking round Île-Grande, it's the grey and salty days that please me best.

Like once last week . . .

A westerly wind was sweeping rain all over the coast. I went first down the Chemin du Gwaker in the direction of Trébeurden, along by Keravel, 'the house of the winds', then down farther to the corniche: the isle of Millau off the coast there dashed with spray. Therafter I went through Trébeurden, and followed the coast road along the beach of Goas Treiz ('the marshy beach'), by Toëno, to Île Grande (in Breton, E*nez Veur*), the 'Big Island'.

Just over a kilometre from north to south, and two kilometres from east to west, the Big Island is accompanied by a whole host of smaller islands such as Losket, Aganton (known familiarly as 'Canton'), Molène, Enez Vran (Crow Island), Enez Erc'h (Snow Island). Then there are the White Rocks (*Kerreg Gwen*), the Comb Reef (*Ar Grib*) and, farther off, across the Goulmeder Pass, the Seven Islands, and across the Kanal Dreoger, the Triagoz. The Enez Veur used to be a real island, like the others, but in the 1950s, a bridge was built to make communications easier with the rest of the country. The Big Island people still get, however, the reputation of being insular and wild, inveterate wreckers and smugglers in the past, still a bit 'apart'.

If, with the intention of walking round the island, you turn right once you're off the bridge, you'll see a handful of boats either straight on their stilts or lopsided on one flank, in the bed of the river. Thereafter, it's a stretch of marshy ground with, here and there, the rusty skeletons of farm implements. Then you're down through dune grass to Toull-Gwenn with its yellow sand and its silver-grey mud, and, over the water, the island of Aval.

Aval island is where Morgane the fairy woman (Morgwenn, 'white sea', daughter of the foam) is supposed to have lived, and where, according to the tradition, King Arthur lies buried. So much lousy literature and corny poetry have accumulated about the figure of Arthur that one is tempted to leave the whole affair alone, but maybe we should consider the story a bit, at least in the by-going.

Arthur was a little prince of Dumnonia (his wife was Gwenn Arc'hant, 'Silver White', and his favourite, Brangwenn, 'White Breasts') who fought against the Saxons, and died about AD 540 – well, he disappeared (maybe Morgane made him invisible, or turned him into a crow . . .). His disappearance corresponds with the emigration of so many island Bretons to Armorica in France, Galicia in Spain and Minho in Portugal. They took the memory of him and turned it into a a cosmic myth, hearing his army in the storm-wind, seeing it in the clouds and imagining Arthur sitting up on the Great Bear or playing his harp on Lyra . . . It's pretty obvious how much imagination and myth is consolation, compensation. When it's tied in with a dogma, you get religion. In other circumstances, we might have had Arthurianity in place of Christianity.

Let's come back to the wind and the walking.

Long lines of seaweed. White splatches of gull-shit on the sand. Rocks covered with whelks and limpets. Still pools full of obscure life. And here a colony of terns at the tide's edge, fluttering in the air every time a bigger wave comes surfing in, to avoid getting their neat little arses wet.

If the Big Island has been known mainly for its granite, especially the type called 'blue granite', tons of which have been hewn off to make pavements in Paris and Bordeaux (the excavations have left amphitheatres for gull concerts among the rocks), every bit of earth has delicate growths. Around the dry-stone walls and in the fields behind them, you come across clusters of whin, in bloom all the year round: pale yellow in winter, full yellow in summer. And alongside it you'll find wild rose, blue thistles, ferns, daisies, buttercups, hyacinths, wild pinks, spurge.

Beyond Toull-Gwenn, you clamber over a rocky section till you encounter a little harbour. Then it's moor, with Crow Rock off shore, till you skirt a wood, after which a large vista opens out, over towards Trébeurden and the Île Millau. You arrive then at the Bird Station, where, among other activities, they gather in birds that have been the victims of oil-slick, and, when they can, nurse them back to normal: in the pen there, stalks a big blue-eyed gannet that looks as if he'll be able to take off again any day now, by his side a little puffin that still looks a bit groggy. Further on, you come to the port, with the cadavers of old boats lining its edge and younger vessels bobbing at anchor. After that, you arrive at a marsh where the migrating birds like to feed: woodcocks, redshanks. Then it's the first houses of the village: Ker José, Ty-ma-Bro, Port d'Attache . . .

Walking through the lanes of the village the first days I was in the district, I was surprised to come across a Rue Joseph Conrad.

It took only a very little research for me to learn that Conrad had actually lived on the island, in 1896. It was the time when Captain Kerseniovski, with *Almayer's Folly* and *An Outcast of the Islands* behind him, and *The Nigger of the Narcissus* ahead of him, was really turning into the writer Joseph Conrad. He had married Miss Jessie George. They had decided to spend their honeymoon on the continent, and he was looking for a quiet place to get on with his work. From St Malo they moved down to Lannion, and there, Conrad was told he would find a house to let on Île-Grande. He spent all in all six months there, from April to September, writing stories such as *An Outpost of Progress* that were to go into the collection *Tales of Unrest*:

'Then, suddenly, he fell asleep, or thought he had slept; but at any rate there was a fog, and somebody had whistled in the fog. He stood up. The day had come, and a heavy mist had descended upon the land: the mist penetrating, enveloping and silent.'

In the *Outpost*, Conrad was talking about Africa. But the general feeling, as well as elements of the description I've quoted, came also,

obviously enough, from his surroundings there on Île-Grande. I read
the tale one afternoon as mist curled at the window of the *Bar de
l'Espérance*.

The Bird Station on the Big Island is connected to Rouzic, one of the
Seven Islands, which is a bird sanctuary. At one point, I was able to
obtain permission to visit it.

This is where the earth-paths turn to sea-paths.

It was late August. We left Ploumanac'h harbour in the fishing
smack belonging to Rougoulouarn, called Rougou, the island guardian. As we came out the Ploumanac'h channel, a rosy haze covered
the horizon. The sea wasn't running too heavy, but big dollops of
water nevertheless came sweeping in over the bow. What with the
noise of the sea, the wind and the throbbing of the engine, I only got
the gist of what Rougou was saying. He was regretting the old days of
fishing, when the sea was full of mackerel ('the blue fish', he called it).
He'd been out that morning, and had caught only fourteen on his
line, hardly enough to supply the fish-stall his wife ran at Perros.
Inshore fishing was on the way out. There were big boats on the
prowl everywhere, carrying forty kilometres of net: with excessive
fishing of that kind, they'd emptied the sea . . .

Rouzic is about four sea miles out.

Rougou anchored ten yards off the rocky shore, and we put out a
little zodiac. Once on shore, we scrambled up to the shoulder of the
island. At the top, the smell of gannet was strong, the grass of the
cliff had been worn away, and there was down floating in the air.
Everywhere gannets (the puffins, petrels and penguins all had gone):
mature fellows with absolutely white black-tipped wings, and dark
little fluffy yunkers. High above, the slow-moving chaos of the
birds, and the *krech-krech* of their cry: they too would be leaving
soon. Some would go as far as Senegal. They'd be back on Rouzic in
January.

It was while coming back from Île-Grande one evening, on the road to Trébeurden, that I saw one of the most amazing sights I've ever witnessed. It was a flock of starlings, no, a *swarm* of starlings, there were thousands of them, flying over the marshes of Quellen. It was the evolutions that were breathtaking: all kinds of whorlings and windings, sudden breaks followed by just as sudden groupings. At times the mass would be sparse and grey, then it would concentrate into a dense black ball before whirling off again into other shapes. The birds seemed to settle finally with the setting sun.

Earth-paths, sea-paths, sky-paths, the body-mind loves them all, and travels along them, into a deeper and deeper reality.

A Garden

It's April again. White blossoms coming out on the cherry tree, and the birches bearing fresh green leaves and pods chockful of yellow pollen . . . A grey sparrow has been perched some time there in that cherry tree, as though posing for a Chinese painter, but now it has whirred off to the mimosa.

I find it hard to exaggerate the delights of a garden.

There are some who make fun of garden-lovers. I came across an example of this recently in the only book by Louis Aragon I can still read, *Le Paysan de Paris* (I was rereading it the other day in the train). 'Those who have travelled all their lives,' he says, 'those who have encountered love in all climates, those who have had their beards singed in the south and their hair frozen in the north, those whose skin bears traces of all the suns and winds of the earth, come home at last with a parrot on their shoulders and one single ambition: have a garden.' Aragon considers and stigmatises this as a sign of resignation and near dotage. I can hardly agree. Age *may* have something to do with it. I'm remembering here the old Japanese saying: 'In youth a man plays with women, in middle age with the arts, and in old age with a garden.' But I don't think it's that simple. Instead of that chronological order (close to the Hindu order, which reserves seclusion for the end of life), a more complete life will make many elements coincide. So I'll go rather to that old Arab text where Allah says: 'Between the chair from which I speak and my tomb, there is a garden.' And to Francis Bacon who, in his *Essays Civil and Moral*, says of gardens: 'God Almighty first planted a garden. And, indeed, it is the purest of human pleasures. It is the greatest refreshment to the spirits of man.' While we're on civility, morality and, why not, philosophy and politics, let us recall Candide's concluding words to Pangloss: 'One must cultivate one's garden.' And if Karl Marx had continued working in the garden of Epicurus, where he wrote his first thesis, who knows, the twentieth century might not have been so noisy and full of conflict, and might really have got out of the nineteenth-century hell.

The other day in Paris, I was asked again, as often happens: 'When's your next trip?' I said I had no particular travelling plans at the moment. 'You're getting old' was the immediate retort. That may be so; indeed, no doubt it is so. But maybe it's more interesting to say I'm getting more and more concentrated. I haven't given up travelling, far from it, I know that. But it's true I'm cultivating more and more my garden, at least in the metaphorical sense.

When, in the course of my work, I feel like a little circumambulatory meditation, I go for a walk round the garden . . .

The garden here isn't a big garden, but it's big enough, you can get a good walk out of it. So, while the states with their banners and cannons are bickering about their identities and pretentions, I sit here quietly, in this granite corner of the galaxy, just looking around.

From the stone steps of my workhouse out, it's first of all on the New Zealand linen-bush that my eye rests: its long spear-blade leaves, dark-red and green, frayed at the tips, crissing in the wind. At other times, according to season, my attention will be given to the Spanish orange-blossom, the white starry flowers of the Philadelphia Virgin, the Korean chrysanthemums, the Californian poppies with their beautiful orange-yellow, the full flush of the rhododendron, the deep redolent blue of the iris, the white and pink and dark-winered of the erigeron from Mexico that can grow in any cranny, the tall Japanese grasses tossing in the bright sea-wind, or the little leaves of the birch trees yellow-specked with autumn.

A garden is a medley of perfumes, a harmony of primary and secondary colours, a co-ordination of forms. It is also, or can be, a kind of world-tour. In this garden here, there are about four hundred plants in all, some of them quite rare – given the right location and the right care, they can all thrive. That's because the climate here is temperate and maritime, with very little frost, and that never long lasting. True, there are the winds. But you can plant a hedge, and rig up supports for your trees when they're young, and have recourse to a lot of tough seaboard plants, some of which may even *like* the wind (the *amenophiles*, as the botanists call them).

If the garden is a world-tour, it's also a kind of map. Here, there are three zones (not counting the yard): the 'back country' zone, concentred on its grove of birches; the 'open field' zone which, plant after plant, leads the eye out on to the valley and the seacoast; and the little 'monk's garden', which is the most protected part, especially since we planted an extra hedge against the west.

The winds were a problem, but a problem that was solved in time.

Then there were the rabbits. Those rascally little fellows kept invading the garden, having a go at every young plant in sight. They obviously considered our garden as a larder of luxury, so luxurious they could afford to just nibble a little at one plant after the other, according to their whim. Something had to be done, we had to come to some kind of *modus vivendi*. I certainly didn't want to set traps. After I'd inquired around, the advice I was given was to rig up a string soaked with an evil-smelling substance that would put the rabbits off. So, from stick to stick, I ran a thick string well soaked, only to find not only that it wasn't very effective, but that one little blighter had decided to come in from the fields, string or no, and set up house *inside* the garden. I caught him one afternoon in my jacket and took him over to the nearby wood. Once there, I unfolded the jacket. Out came Jack, standing still, nose twitching, looking round. He then decided it was a better life inside the jacket and took refuge in one of the sleeves. I nudged him out of it, and waited till he felt ready to venture into the new world. He took his time, his beady little eyes sizing up the situation. Then he took a little hip-hop that landed him in ivy. He sniffed at it, nibbled at it, then bounded off into the big dark wood.

It was only when the garden became the territory of Catou that the rabbits decided to call it a day and flit to a non-cat area.

We'd been told that if we got a cat, we wouldn't have any birds. Well, that's not true. Maybe that's because Catou, the cat of the house, is a well-fed cat that can afford, with some exceptions, to contemplate birds without being overcome with the desire to devour them.

There are sparrows galore here, a whole parliament of them, and starlings click-clicking on the chimney stack, or lined along the telephone wires, and magpies, and crows, and gulls and jays (that blue-brown streak and the shriek!) and wee jenny wrens and swallows and blackies and thrushes and tomtits, and redbreasts, and many another.

It was a late evening in August, a golden sun flooding coast, valley and house. I was sitting quietly in my writing-room, when I heard a 'tap-tap, tap-tap-tap' at the window. That was Magpie, introducing himself. Of all the birds here it was the magpies who struck me most in the early days. Simply because I'd never seen them in such numbers before. There were so many of them that I immediately thought of the Chemin du Gwaker as Magpie Road. There are always several of them in the garden. A man who came to pay me a visit in the first days said he didn't like magpies. I can't understand statements like that. Is it because, with their glossy coat and tails, they look so immaculately elegant? Is it because they fly with a mechanical kind of whirr? Or is it because they have a reputation for stealing, or for picking out the eyes of lambs and piglets? In China, on the contrary, magpies are con-sidered as birds of good omen. In fact, the Chinese word for magpie means, literally, 'bird of joy'. It's a specially good omen if a magpie builds its nest near your house. Well, in the second year of our residence here, a couple of magpies built their nest in the old apple-tree – how closer could you get? I felt grateful to them. I like to hear them *tchak-a-tchak-a-tchaking* from morning till night.

There's a Navajo song that says the magpie bears in its wings 'the whiteness of dawn'.

It was on 20 September that the travelling pigeon turned up. There it was, under the cherry tree, soft-grey on back and breast, iridescently violet at the neck, with a ring on either leg. We gave it some millet right away, and it ate with great application. On the following days, we kept putting the millet on that same spot. Sometimes we'd see it perched on the chimney of the old house, sometimes on the ridge of my work-house. Every now and then it would take a little flight of about forty yards and then come back, often alighting on the house of our neighbour across the road as a half-way stage. I know very little about pigeons. But I've heard about people who will travel with them to some spot, and then leave them to make their own way home: it's a kind of sport, at times, I think, competitive. I suppose this was the case with our pigeon. Maybe some Scotsman had taken him down to Spain, or some Spanishman had taken him up to Scotland. On his way, he must have got tired, and had stopped for a rest. That's what the postman said. He sometimes found one in his garden, and it left in one or two days. Ours stayed a day, then another day, then a third day, a fourth day . . . I could imagine that pigeon saying to itself: 'I've had enough of all this racing caper, to hell with my so-called owner, I'm staying right here.' The only trouble was Catou. Well-fed or no, when he realised one day there was a pigeon in the vicinity within reach of his paw, he took up elaborate hunting positions, stretched out flat, waiting, ready to leap, clutch and claw. I tried to reason with him, to no effect. Marie-Claude then tried to distract his attention with some cat-milk. But even that was no go. It was only when the pigeon, becoming aware that something was amiss, flew to the chimney, that Catou thought he'd make do with the milk. I just hoped the pigeon would always be smart enough to flutter off at the right moment. I was really getting used to him. And then, after five days, all of a sudden, he left. After he'd gone, I felt his absence. But there was some consolation in thinking of him flying strong with the wind, somewhere along the coast, all alone. Maybe we'd see him the following year, well, some other year . . .

She sits there like some old goddess of the rain and mud. A kind of antediluvian Venus. I'm talking about a toad. No description of Gwenved's garden would be complete without her. I see her every now and then. Sometimes on the steps to my study, at other times on the threshold of the main house. It's there she is tonight, an evening in early July, and rose petals shaken by the sea-wind falling all around her. She doesn't budge an inch, warty old Venus in the midst of a shower of rose petals. I give her a wink, and I'm not sure she isn't winking back. I have the distinct impression that she has one eye open and one eye closed. But, of course, I could be wrong.

There are big glass surfaces on the buildings of the house here. The result is that a small bird – sparrow, finch, tit or thrush – will now and then bang into them, mistaking reflection for a continuation of the landscape. Mostly, even in those cases, they're just stunned, lie still for a moment, then skim off again. But not always. Sometimes the thump is fatal. All I can do then is pick up the body, maybe with a blob of blood at the beak, and take it up to the north-west corner of the garden. That's where the bird cemetery is. There's a dyke up there with biggish stones embedded in the earth. I remove a stone, scrape out a little hollow, line it with ivy leaves, lay the bird in it carefully, cover it with earth, and then put the stone back in place. I put up no signs. No one would know this is a cemetery. I don't say much either. But I feel I've done at least the best I can.

I did the same with a young bat that had fallen from its nest overlooking the 'monk's garden'. I picked it up and realised from a very vague twitching it was still alive, just barely alive. I took it into the house, the little mousey grey body with the great ears that can capture ultrasounds, the fine complex texture of the wings. Marie-Claude fetched a dropper, and let a drop of water fall into the little creature's mouth. That seemed to give it a last lease of life. It trembled all over, stretched its beautiful wings, and was dead.

So, death is part of the garden too. But while knowing it, I don't harp on it. And when I look out over the grasses and flowers and trees, it's not primarily of death I think. Nor of life for that matter. I see what I see, that's all.

THE GREAT WORLD
OF LITTLE CATOU

Strange as it seems now, for long I did not know what the presence of a cat can mean. I had read about cats. I had especially liked, when I was a kid, that story by Rudyard Kipling about the cat that walked by himself: '. . . he is the cat that walks by himself, and all places are alike to him. Then he goes out to the Wet Wild Woods or up the Wet Wild Trees or on the Wet Wild Roofs, waving his wild tail and walking by his wild lone.' But I'd forgotten about that story. It's only here in Brittany I've begun to collect all the cat texts I can get my hands on.

At least two writers, one in Japan and one in France (two of the most cultured countries in the world, *n'est-ce pas?*), have written whole books about a cat: I'm thinking of Natsume Sôseki's *Wagahai wa neko de aru* ('I am a Cat') and *Rroû* by Maurice Genevoix.

Sôseki lived at a time when Japanese men walked through the streets of Tokyo in kimonos and bowler hats, their minds torn between east and west, between Japanese tradition and Euro-American modernity. One serious proposal was that the Japanese language should be abandoned altogether, and that everybody should speak English. Sôseki learned English, but without forgetting Japanese. After four years in England, he came back to Japan in 1903 to take over the chair of English literature at the Imperial University of Tokyo. It was while teaching there that he wrote the text, usually called a novel, about a cat. But it's not really a novel, not even a story, it's a series of scenes, with no plot or obvious sequence, that in fact makes feline fun of the novel. Each scene is packed with extravagant reference, comic cogitation, social observation, in an anarchic disorder. Through it all, sardonic and self-contained, stalks a nameless cat who takes a cool look at humanity from the outside. What he sees, and Sôseki through his eyes, is the brutal disruption of a subtle order, the takeover of a culture by ignorant industrialists and vulgar businessmen, while poet-intellectuals such as his master become more and more marginalised, finally shutting themselves up 'like bad-tempered oysters', and perhaps going slowly mad. Sôseki doesn't go mad, probably thanks to his cat. If he uses black humour, and has the occasional thought of suicide, he survives, not by tragic vociferation or by lolling about in sentimental slush, but by the free play of a sensitive mind – something, shall we say, like the movements of a cat.

Maurice Genevoix, for his part, came back from the 14–18 war with a horror of it all that he expressed in a series of war-books. But mainly, at least for me, he tried from then on to get in touch with what he called 'the true world' via the country scenes and animal life of the Loire valley. *Rroû*, the story of a black cat with green eyes (*rroû* is the throaty sign he makes), is one of his best pieces. For Sôseki, his cat was mainly a device for him to make comments. In *Rroû*, Genevoix really goes into the life of a cat and follows his wanderings, step by step, through the fields and woods. In the end, Rroû leaves human society altogether. The book comes to a close with the vision of his green eyes wide open and gleaming in the darkness of a non-human night . . .

The old Celtic literature is full of the association between men and animals – Ernest Renan, one of my spiritual neighbours, draws attention to it in an essay, mentioning the blackbird of Cilgwri, the deer of Redyuvre, the owl of Cwm Cawlwyd, the eagle of Gwern Abwy, and the salmon of Llyn Llaw. But the most re-knowned example (reknowned, that is, among us Celtic animal-lovers) is the old poem about the scholar-writer and his cat Pangur Ban (Pangur the White), who would always be with him in the scriptorium:

> *Though we toil for days and years*
> *Neither one the other hinders*
> *Each is highly skilled and hence*
> *Enjoys his work in total silence*
>
> *Within his paws the fate of mice*
> *He keeps himself in daily practice*
> *I too, making dark things clear*
> *Am of my trade a perfect master*

Catou is a black cat with golden eyes. After this cursory and preliminary approach, though, you see that, on his breast, the black shades into a rich chestnut brown, and that in the midst of the black brown there's a white patch known as the 'angel's mark' (which, in the Middle Ages, was enough to save a cat from being burnt alive by certain ghoul-haunted creeps who had persuaded themselves that cats were diabolical and up to all kinds of witchery).

It was Marie-Claude who invented the name Catou. I like it a lot – so, I think, does Catou (he would, I am sure, have growled in protest at 'Napoleon' or turned away in disdain from 'Snooky'). 'Catou' is at one and the same time generic (cat is cat – not substitute or plaything) and intimate. It's also nice to pronounce, whether as a whispered caress, or as a loud halloo when he's away in the wilds somewhere and hasn't turned up.

When Catou arrived here at Gwenved, he was only two months old, and he had caught a chill. Every now and then the little chap would sneeze, and his big eyes were watering a bit. I've never seen him with a cold since, so I conclude that either he has developed a strong constitution, or that it's only pussycats that have colds.

The first thing that struck me about Catou is that he's a creature of the threshold, of the in-between-two-areas. His great pleasure is to be half-in, half-out, rump in the warmth of the house, snitch sniff-sniffing at the cool air of the outside. Then, he's able to enjoy every little snippet of time. Even thirty seconds in a good position, he'll take it, indulge in it to the full, ready to bound away to another one at the slightest disturbance or attraction. If he sometimes takes time to make up his mind, at others I'm astonished at the quickness of his changes.

The way he moves is amazing. One hears praises of dancers, male and female, excited commentators expatiate on their trials and triumphs. But nothing in all that art can give me as much pleasure as to see Catou simply going about his daily occupations. Consider the way he'll fling up a leg doing his toilet. Absolute unconscious grace! Look at the way he'll place himself on any square of cloth or paper lying around: paws primly posed, totally at ease. If there was a stamp on the floor, Catou would manage to position his little arsehole right in the middle of it, and look around with an expression of bland contentment. And see how he stretches himself, with great conscientiousness and enjoyment, putting one paw forward, then the other, thereupon raising up his rear end, and pushing, before doing the same thing frontward. I love too watching him cleaning up his claws on the bark of the old apple-tree, in a frenzy of pleasure. Every now and then, Catou will shin up that apple-tree, and show off. He'll go from trunk to branch, and from branch to branchlet, and from branchlet to twig, showing us what he can do by way of balance and acrobatics. He'll pause to make sure we're looking. He really is showing off, putting on a demonstration, because when we stop looking and move off, down he comes.

I've got a pretty good idea of Catou's territory. I realised where it ended the first time he came with us for a walk along the Gwaker road. At one point, he got worried, started even mewing a bit, which is rare for Catou: he's no habitual mewer; he's a silent-type cat. But there he was actually *mewing*, and sticking closer to us than usual. So, his habitual territory extends a few hundred yards around the house.

I'd be very curious to follow Catou on his nightly prowls. I wonder where he goes, what he does. Once he turned up in the morning bedecked in pig shit (there it was pretty obvious he'd paid a visit to Loïc Rannou's farm). But that morning he got such a washdown (something he definitely does *not* like) that he's probably scored that one off his list. There is, however, no lack around of mousey corners, and moley hills, not to speak of all kinds of sweet-smelling, wild-smelling plants, flowers, bushes and trees.

I'd like Catou to always stay in the garden. There's plenty of room there, and all kinds of interestingly different areas. But he just has to go farther afield. At times, in the past, it would be across the road and down by the apple-trees. At other times, it'd be the cow-patch, where he'd sniff around, and take refuge in the hawthorn hedge when it rained, and gaze out from there with his big golden eyes (extraordinary golden eyes that take on now and then a weird green glimmer).

Catou! Catou! – when we call him from the kitchen door, we like to see him come bounding over the adjacent fields. Sometimes, we have to call him more than once. Maybe he hasn't heard, or is very far away? Maybe he has important business on hand ? The horrible thought is always there too that he could get run over by some careless fool in a car, or get killed by a hunter; one of them told me one day he shot cats on sight: he didn't like them because they hunted his rabbits. So there's worry, even if we don't say anything.

But, look, here he comes, loping along the edge of the maize field.

'Hello, Catou, little pal Catou!'

When he comes in from an outing, by day or by night, his fur smells of the outdoors. He wears the outdoors on him, probably at the tip of every single hair. Sometimes, though, he'll have taken a rollabout on the road or in some dry corner of the garden so that when I half-caress, half-pat him, the dust comes off in clouds. After a dirty, but no doubt very satisfying rollabout like that, he'll think nothing, of course, of settling down on exquisite, immaculate silk.

When I open the shutters in the morning, I most often don't have to call, he's heard the movement inside and knows it's opening time. While the shutter is rolling up, he moves around in a circle, and opens his mouth in a silent mew. In then he comes and rubs against my legs, before making, with a throaty little growl, which is a kind of greeting, for the back kitchen, where his plate is ready.

Breakfast consists in cracknels. Catou has got into the habit of asking too for something extra, and he usually gets it: maybe one or two bits of cheese, or more recently, some special cat-milk he's crazy about. He has a way of asking that is irresistible: he'll look deeply at you, licking his black lips with his little rough pink tongue, now and then opening his jaws, but without making a sound.

After breakfast, with the trimmings, satisfied (when Catou has enjoyed something, you know it: he tries to capture every last degree of pleasure by licking his chops in long tongue-curling delight), he decides exactly where he's going to sleep. He has several possibilities: various chairs and armchairs, the sofa, the little bed in Marie-Claude's study . . . And goes to sleep, his nose hidden in his paws.

'Have a good sleep, little chap.'

At such words, Catou will sometimes open up a quarter of an eye, as if to say: 'Don't worry about that, pal, see you later.'

I love to watch him yawn. Then I see his rough pink little tongue, and clean sharp fangs, one a bit broken, and his leathery lips that have a dark-grey ancientness to them, and the ridged roof of his mouth. He yawns a lot. Sometimes, when he opens his mouth to say something like: 'Anything nice today?', he changes his mind in the middle of the process and makes a good, long yawn of it.

I know Catou sometimes has a fight. Because every now and then, there'll be a patch of fur missing, and one of his ears is slightly tattered. I've seen him in action. There was this other cat adopted by the neighbours across the road: a Siamese with a skellie eye and one ear missing, a real old-timer. He was on the road one day, and Catou, stiffening and crouching, saw him coming. He eyed him from ten yards away, six yards, three . . . The other kept advancing, on the other side of the road, glancing at Catou every so often, not wanting to pay much attention, though, because if he didn't pay attention, who knows, maybe Catou wouldn't either. Three yards, one yard, level – and the other cat's past. It's then that Catou makes his move. Chases that other cat into the neighbour's garden, and maybe farther, but by this time I've lost them from sight. They seemed in the end to have come to some kind of arrangement, however, the two of them, because, later, I'd sometimes see Catou eyeing the other cat going about his business, saying nothing.

When the old forty-niner died or moved on, the neighbours got another cat, a little black one, almost the exact replica of Catou, whom they called Waldo. Waldo was (he ate poison in a field a year later) a very nice little cat, but, at the beginning at least, he had no sense of territory at all and he'd not only walk all over Catou's grounds, he'd imitate him in every single movement. If Catou sat on one step, little Waldo would sit in exactly the same position on another step. And he'd keep following Catou around. Catou was obviously annoyed, but he was patient.

I love to see him sitting quiet on the window ledge, watching the raindrops slither down the panes. Now and then his shoulders will twitch a bit. And every now and then, when something has really awaked his attention, he cranes his neck, ears stretched high, holds that position for a while, then settles back.

One spring, he had a long relationship with a tit there at the window. The little tit would come every day at the same hour to play on the branch of a rose-bush that crossed the window. At the beginning, Catou would grit his teeth and get down ready to pounce. He did even pounce now and then, for a few days. But pretty soon he gave it up. The tit seemed also to begin to realise there was no danger. It went about its acrobatics while Catou looked on contemplatively, innocence personified, looking as if he'd never hurt a fly. In fact, he never hurts a fly. If he's crouched or couched at the glass door of the kitchen and a fly turns up, he just follows it with his eyes, interested, but no more than that.

Catou can be totally, sublimely indifferent. But if once he decides to be interested, there's nobody more interested than Catou. I don't let him in often to the workshop, because there are piles of paper in

there that even a careful cat could tumble down. So he's not in here
often, but he is now and then. And he's interested – oh, is he *interested*.
The smell of books and ink and paper! And those deep shelters you
can go right into the back of and look out from . . .

As will have become obvious by this time, I love Catou. Oh, that
may be a silly thing to say and if he knew, Catou probably wouldn't
give a damn. His kind have been around a longer time than mine,
and their attitudes are different. Then there's that absolute solitude
of his. Catou is no pet. He has all the splendid independence of a
semi-wild cat. Nevertheless, there are times, when he's snuggled
down beside me, with one of his paws resting on my arm, I feel we
have something like an intimate relationship. He likes when I caress
his head too – sometimes he'll come asking for it, pushing his head
up against my hand. But not always, and never too much. Sometimes
when I want to caress him, he'll slink down close to the ground and
slip away out of my touch. At times too he'll use his fangs and his
claws, as warning. I've felt him with his teeth just held on my skin,
not sinking in. Though it *has* happened, especially in his younger
days, when I approached him at the wrong moment, that he drew
blood. I never minded that, I just put it down to my human
stupidity.

Catou obviously enjoys his territory so much, gazing here, sniff-
sniffing there, that when, at times, I leave Gwenved on some trip,
which may be more or less voluntary, I feel not only a sense of
separation, but something deeper than that: a kind of despair that I've
let the territory down, haven't lived enough up to it – a kind of
disgust at the careless superficiality of so much human life.

Down in the library this morning I took a book of philosophy from
the shelves. As I flipped through the pages, I came across one that
stopped me. I saw that, reading it for the first time, I had sketched on
that page Catou's face. From that arduous text emerges Catou's face,

with his pointed ears, his big eyes and his delicate, oh so very delicate nose.

It's pretty obvious to me that for years now I've been looking for a kind of thinking and writing that goes round the world the way a cat goes round its territory.

The Letter-box

W e've just set up a new letter-box, outside the gate, beside one of the granite pillars: dark green metal, regulation postal size. The previous one should have lasted a lifetime, but one morning, a first of January, when brains are often a bit blurred, somebody using our parking to turn about in backed his car plumb into the box. That left it squee-gee, but still usable. The squee-geeness, however, gradually got worse and the whole box slowly went agley. A few weeks back, the door just wouldn't shut any more. We used the old and gaping box for a while – fortunately there was no rain blowing in from the east those days. Then we finally got round to buying this brand-new one and setting it up.

It's a pretty big box and it holds a lot of stuff. Before bringing the mail into the house, I stop at the tool-shed, where the dustbin sits, and dump in it all the increasingly thick wad of bumph: the glossy adverts, the Personalised Letters from this or that commercial firm telling you that you have just won ten million francs.

After that, I come into the house, take a knife from the kitchen drawer, and, settling down at the table, begin opening.

Among the letters, there will be the occasional complaining, recriminating, sometimes insulting one about, say, manuscripts I haven't acknowledged the receipt of, and haven't returned: 'Three years ago, after a talk you did in Boulogne, I handed over to you a manuscript entitled *Murder in the Bay*. All I wanted from you was for you to tell me where I could get it published. If you have nothing to offer me, please return the manuscript at once . . .' OK, OK Has the guy included stamps? No, of course not. Anyway, that's not the main thing. What really bothers me is that by this time, that manuscript (an 'oceanic detective novel') will be lying under a hundred others of its kind, it'll be a mining job to extract it, and, in addition, I'll have to pack it up and take it to the post.

For manuscripts sent to me, I worked out at one time what I felt was quite a neat little circular letter. It went like this:

'Thanks for your manuscript and for the confidence you thereby show in me. But for the last few years, I've been receiving so much mail and manuscripts that it's difficult for me to handle it all while getting on with my own work. However I do my best and, without promising to write back, I shall try to do so. I hope you'll understand the situation. All best wishes on your way.'

But either I forget to send it, or I send it along as a pilot to a screed I've spent three hours on.

Anyway, not all the letters in the mail are like that one. In fact, that kind is rare. Most are substantial and interesting. But to answer a good letter like that takes a lot of time. So I tend to set them aside, saying to myself I'll let the answer accumulate in my brain and wait for the appropriate moment. I do that with really good intentions. And I end up writing a lot of letters this way, maybe a thousand or so a year. But others *pile up*. I know it would make good sense to set aside a period every day for letter writing. But I've never been able to adopt that reasonable policy. It would mean interrupting the natural flow.

The result, for long, was a latent bad conscience, even faint traces of chronic anxiety.

I use to waken up at three in the morning, with a voice repeating over and over in my brain: 'You haven't written to X; you haven't answered Y; don't forget the reply to Z.'

I've got over that a bit – just a bit.

The process of healing went from anxiety to despair, from despair to resignation, from resignation to a cool conviction that the best letters I can write are my books.

But the cure is only partial, and I have relapses.

Because the letters *keep piling up*.

At the moment of writing this, I've got a Himalaya on the floor, a Caucasus in the north-east corner of the room, and there's a Great Wall of China at the left of my table.

At one point, so as to get at least some order into the accumulation, I decided to be really efficient about it. So I got hold of three big boxes, and set them up on a shelf, marking them: 'URGENT', 'AS IT COMES', 'MAYBE'. I sorted out piles of mail for a whole week. But maybe because the sorting itself had exhausted me, or because I'd salved my conscience a little, or because I'd achieved at least some technical satisfaction (I'm open to all hypotheses), I left it at that, and the boxes remained full.

Every now and then, so as to clear the decks a little and not feel totally smothered, I have to do something radical: I put hundreds and hundreds of letters into cardboard boxes, mark them 'UNCLASSI-

FIED', 'UNANSWERED', and stack them away in the store house, addressed to the twenty-ninth century.

What I'm writing here is maybe a kind of Open Letter, with thanks and apologies, to all those people whose letters have been read with interest and pleasure, but who, despite not only my good intentions but my real desire, have never received an answer.

There are all kinds of letters that give me pleasure and awaken my curiosity.

There are those that tell me about a person's life, the paths he or she is following. The other day, for example, came a letter from a young Belgian, resident in Brussels, just back from a trip to the Frisian Islands and Heligoland, where his ancestors, seamen and merchants, had lived and worked. He told me about the trip, about life in Brussels, about 'the Toone theatre', with its characters Jos and Jef, and Waltje, 'the little French-speaking Belgian'. And he got on then to language, telling me about his interest in *le burgonsche* and about the words he heard on the Ardennes plateau, where he liked to go for walks: for example, *grabouilleux*, for 'twisted' – referring to trees . . .

Somebody else writes me from a monastery in the Morvan. He says he knows I'm not a Christian, and that I'm not too interested in theology. But he wants me to know that as a Christian who has studied theology pretty thoroughly, he reads my texts – so, he says, do a lot of monks. Most literature and poetry, including literature and poetry professedly Christian, hardly awaken his interest, because they nowhere approach the field in which he feels he is implicated. He goes to monasteries, mostly in the Morvan, in the Ardèche and in Brittany, because they offer him a space he can't find elsewhere in society. But even the monasteries are being invaded. The monks have to put up increasingly with hordes of nutcases, their heads either screaming blue murder or full of syncretic mush. Only the other night, they had to drive one away from the altar in the chapel, where, stark naked, he was performing a ritualistic kind of home-made rumba . . . This man is also a fisherman. He tells me about the migration of sea-trout from the North Sea up the rivers of Normandy. The fish don't eat much on the trip, and live on the mineral salts in their scales. That's why they turn silver white at those times, so that the sea-trout is locally called *la blanche* ('the white one'). When he's caught a fish, my correspondent tells me, he sends its scales to a laboratory in Rennes for analysis, so he knows, for example, how many times it's made the migration. He enters all these data in a notebook that also contains poems composed during solitudinous moments on riverbanks. This letter ends with an evocation of St Anthony, preaching to people on the Calabrian coast. They wouldn't listen to him. 'Very well,' said Anthony, 'if that's the way you want it, I'll go off down the shore and preach to the fish.' At that very moment, the sea became white with shoals of fish approaching.

Then, there are the letters about the paths and by-paths of literature.

A couple of weeks back, a letter came in from Marseilles telling me about a writer I might be interested in. 'Oh, not a great writer, certainly,' said my correspondent, but one who maybe managed to capture, here and there, something of the 'poetry of the sea'. This was Louis Brauquier, born in Marseilles in 1900 and who entered the service of the *Messageries Maritimes* in 1924, occupying over the years posts in Sydney, Noumea, Shanghai, Saigon, Colombo and Alexandria. Brauquier's first book of poems was called *Et l'au-delà de Suez* ('beyond Suez', an official term, used in Cairo, to designate all merchandise destined for ports outside the Mediterranean), his second, *Bar de l'escale*, and these were followed by *Pilote*, *Écrits à Shanghaï*. My correspondent underlines in blue a line in one of the poems saying about a ship's captain: 'Imperturbably, he follows his blue road', asking me if by any chance that line had inspired the title of one of my own books. I write back, saying no, that that title had come up out of my unconscious via a vision of the St Lawrence, and telling him that another correspondent, from Barcelona this time, had asked me if my title had anything to do with a book published at Barcelona in Catalan, in 1964, by Joseph M. de Sagarra: *La Ruta Blava, viatge a les mars del Sud* (the text is dated 1937). Again I'd had to say no, but that the coincidence interested me.

This morning brings a letter from an American who's been twenty years' resident on the Île de Ré. He begins by referring to poem LXXV of Pound's *Cantos*, which consists entirely of a piece of music, preceded by a few lines addressed to one Gerhart. This Gerhart, my American correspondent tells me, was a real person, and he met him on a snowy slope in the Bavarian Alps in the winter of 1946. A brilliant musician, Gerhart had gone to Paris at the age of twenty, then to Italy, staying mainly on Capri. During the war years he was stuck in Germany, refusing to play for Nazi dignitaries, working as a slater. After the war, he and his wife left for California, where he became friends with Henry Miller. Then later again, he went down to Mexico, where he still maybe was, unless he had died.

I go down to the library and get out Pound's *Cantos*. Yes, there's the beginning of Canto LXXV:

> *Out of Phlegethon*
> *out of Phlegethon*
> *Gerhart*
> *art thou come forth out of Phlegethon*
> *with Buxtehude and Klages in your satchel, with the*
> *Ständebuch of Sachs in yr/luggage . . .*

As I read that, it's a moving picture of all the exiles, political and intellectual of the twentieth century that crosses my mind.

There are also letters that ask questions. Big things straight out of the blue.

A couple of days ago, somebody asked me what I thought of Paradise.

Just like that.

My first reaction was to say to myself: it's just a Hollywood concept. But then, I thought, maybe we can go a bit deeper, maybe we can even pinpoint the idea of Paradise in time . . .

Maybe the notion of Paradise – 'Garden of Eden' in the Near-East and in the West, 'Peach Blossom Land' in the farthest East – started up about eleven thousand years ago, with the beginning of agriculture and the domestication of beasts, soon followed by villages, towns, metal tools and weapons. Mankind was proud of itself, lord, or almost, of all it surveyed. It was all set to build up a totally human world.

That meant work. It meant herding and branding animals. It meant the accumulation of goods, followed by the establishment of power-structures. It meant genealogies, eternity-desires, death-obsessions, all this leading into politics and religion combined. It meant loading the landscape with symbols. The world was rolling on the progress road.

Great!

Yet there grew a feeling, a deep-down nagging feeling, that something had been lost.

That's where Paradise comes in.

Traces of the lost world were still there: the wild animals of the woods, the lilies of the field, rhythms other than mechanical repetition . . .

But Paradise was elsewhere.

A dream, an ideal . . .

And systems of thought were built up to explain why it was lost, as well as epic poems to describe the process.

There are libraries full of it all, and minds are still rife with it.

The thing now maybe is to try and get outside the hell–paradise dialectics, get rid of the symbols, the religion, the metaphysics, and try and work out a new relationship with the earth and what grows and lives on it.

That's what I think of when I walk down the valley path to the coast, passing cattle with number plates clamped to their ears, and a grey-brown-black donkey that ambles up to me so I can stroke its forehead, and a white goat, and a red-gold mass of swaying rye (it's late June), till I come to the top of the cliff and look out over the expanse of the bay.

A letter in the box this morning asks me if this place, Gwenved, is going to be my definitive place, or if, in a few years' time, I'll go elsewhere. I really don't know. For the moment, I feel I have almost perfect conditions for living and working the way I want to. Then, this place is strategically well situated: half-way up the continent, and out on a promontory.

That said, our civilisation is such that you're never sure what kind of new aggression or nuisance is liable to turn up. I hate to think what might be done according to certain logics, and I won't talk about them, I wouldn't want to be giving anybody any ideas.

So I sit, like this morning, in the cool and shade and quiet of this library, surrounded by books from all countries and all ages, looking out on to flowers and trees, and the cat lying, paws stretched out, benignly asleep after his last night's rambles.

I don't see myself leaving this place. I can't imagine where else I would go. But you never know.

All kinds of letters, then, from all kinds of people, from all over the world, turn up in the letter-box – showing how books travel, and how a mental network exists outside all the cluttered crap of noisier communication systems. Which is why, despite the little difficulties and inconveniences I evoked at the beginning of this 'letter', far be it for me to curse the mail or damn the post-office. I bless the letter-box!

So, by the way, does Catou. It's one of his favourite observation posts. He springs up on to it and, settling down, head on paws, eyes alert, corresponds with the cosmos.

FROM PLATO
TO PLANKTON

At the beginning of that summer, I got a letter from the
Marine Biology and Oceanology Station at Roscoff (Patrick Geddes,
the Scottish biologist and later sociologist, studied there a century ago),
inviting me to come over and have a drink 'on the other side of Morlaix
Bay'. My correspondent wound up his letter telling me how I was to
find him: 'I live in the so-called Mary Stuart house, but I'm more often
in the laboratory, facing the sea', and he signed it: 'Sylvain Le Gall'.

It was on a fine July afternoon that we left, Marie-Claude and I, to make
the acquaintance of Monsieur Le Gall and the marine biology station.

I knew roughly where it was, at least the new building. Once there, Le Gall had told me, I was to cross the street and I'd find a garden. So cross the street we did, and there, true enough, was a garden: a charming place a bit out of time, with palm-trees growing beside old rusty anchors, amid clusters of exotic flowers.

We found Monsieur le Gall in a spacious common room on the ground floor, where students were drinking coffee and reading up the notes they'd taken in the course of a recent expedition to the shore.

The old marine biology station at Roscoff has a whole series of little laboratories called *stalles*, each of them containing a 'wet board' (*paillasse humide*) with sea-water on tap for the study of specimens, and a 'dry board' (*paillasse sèche*) for reading documents and writing up reports. In one of those *stalles*, said Monsieur Le Gall, a certain young man by the name of Louis Destouches, who later, under the name of Céline, was to be the author of *Voyage au bout de la nuit* ('Journey to the end of night'), had undertaken research on a microscopic type of worm, research that was published, in October 1920, in the official journal of the Academy of Science under the title: 'Physiological observations on *convoluta roscoffensis*'.

'I knew that would interest you,' said Le Gall, opening a refrigerator to show us the object of his own present research: a huge bottle full of a yellowish liquid which he referred to in an offhand way as 'plankton soup'.

After that we went along a labyrinth of wood-panelled corridors to Le Gall's office.
Once there, Le Gall adjusts a microscope, inviting us to have a good long look at a series of diatoms, lovely little delicate golden structures: *rhizosolenia delicatula*. He then takes out the enormous *Atlas der Diatomaceenkunde* by Adolf Schmidt, showing us hundreds of the same family, all with different forms. For years and years, he tells us, researchers have been discovering new structures, and every time they give 'their' diatom a name. That makes for a formidable nomenclature. But they're all plankton.

Playing the pedagogue, not without irony, Monsieur Le Gall proceeds to inform us that there are three types of life in the sea: *plankton*, everything that floats; *nekton*, everything that swims, all the fishes; and *benthos*, the creatures of the deep. It was Hensen, professor of physiology at the university of Kiel, who invented the term 'plankton' (his big Plankton Expedition dates back to 1889). As to the benthos, a new submarine has just been built that will go down six kilometres and have a good look round: 'God only knows what we'll find.' At this very moment, exploration is going on in the seas off Japan. But for phytoplankton, the Roscoff estuary is as good as anywhere, in fact one of the richest zones in the world. That's because it's a natural turbidostat, where physical time (mostly tidal) joins up with biological time (the growth-time of the planktonic seaweed) in an extremely interesting way. What Le Gall and others are studying is the annual cycle of phytoplankton, from the 'spring bloom' on, as well as the hydrodynamics of those geomorphological sites called *rias* and the flow of energy and materials in marine ecosystems.

'Does all that really interest you?'

'Of course, and you know it. Otherwise you wouldn't have invited me.'

Le Gall chuckles.

'I've never come across a poet like you.'

'Oh,' I say, 'there are other fish in the intellectual sea like me, but we haven't been catalogued yet.'

Le Gall chuckles again.

Then, saying that we've had enough of science for the moment, he suggests that we leave the laboratories and go across to Mary Stuart's house, where he's invited a couple of colleagues to have a drink with us. As we quit the station, we pass by the pool where they keep specimens under scrutiny. I see a big flat fish gliding smoothly in the depths.

'A torpedo,' says Le Gall, 'we're studying its electrical discharges.'

When we get into the Mary Stuart house, with its bare walls and spare furniture, Sylvain says that, fine view or not, the snag of the place is that you're liable to die of pneumonia. He does his best to keep it heated: he has a vast stock of wood piled up in a handy corner that was once the toilet (with a hole giving direct access to the sea), but it's no easy job, because the walls are full of cracks. His wife stayed a week and then skeedaddled. So Sylvain is making it alone. I think he finds a certain satisfaction in it, a kind of monastic pleasure.

When his two colleagues turn up, they're accompanied by an Irish biologist from the University of Galway.

'It's the desert of the Tartars here,' says one of the Frenchmen, 'an intellectual fort.'

'An outpost of progress,' says the Irishman.

'A place where weather reports are more important than those of the Stock Exchange,' says the other Frenchman.

Sylvain brings out the whisky.

'Here's to copepods and the Pope,' says the Irishman.

'Here's to Plato and the plankton,' say I.

The conversation goes from the ghost of Mary Stuart, which Sylvain swears he saw scooting out the window the moment he opened the door, to the mystery of copepods; from the chaotic nature of Brittany's north coast ('Navigation here is a real poem') to stories about a Dutch Jesuit who studied the local ants and the shout John Steinbeck let out, a shout that could be heard 'from hell to Bethlehem', when he stepped barefoot on a crab on a beach in Connemara. From there on it continues to the formation of *grauwachs*, to a discussion concerning the origin of the colour violet (from the *murex*? from the *aplysia*?), and the fact that the harsh winter of twenty years back had killed off all the devilfish in the Celtic Sea, after which we pass on to the psychology of *octopus vulgaris*, the proliferation of Japanese sargasso weed in Breton waters, the behaviour of those yellow frogs that go down to the sea at night, the presence off the Irish coast of giant turtles from Florida, the pleasure of 'going down to the tide' every day, and the schizophrenic characteristics of modern civilisation.

There was a pre-schizophrenic West (that of Heraclitus, for example).

And what we have to get at now is a *post*-schizophrenic West.

That, we all agree (the whisky makes for a large consensus), is what, each in his own way, we're all working at.

VISITORS

Having chosen to live in a house on the Breton coast, I was a bit afraid, at the beginning, despite my assiduously cultivating the reputation of a bear (a *polar* bear), that I might get too many unsolicited visits – after all, Brittany is only a few hours out of Paris, which is overrun with slowly suffocating citizens, and I could imagine acquaintances (long-standing friends who know me well are always very discreet) saying to themselves some Friday evening: 'Why not spend a little breather of a weekend in Brittany, pay a visit to the Whites?' Which is why I thought of putting up a couple of notices at the gate: 'Is your journey really necessary?', or 'Beware, explosive

poet!', or again 'Writer at work – non stop'. But on reflection, that
would be really overdoing it, and I preferred to leave things open.
There have been, in fact, some chance visitors I would hate to have
missed!

He came to the gate one afternoon, wearing an orange fisherman's
blouse and a skip cap on his head. I asked him in, but he shook his
head and just handed me a plastic bag full of grey-brown shrimps,
saying: 'A little present from Lannion Bay', and was off. This was
Roparz Gouessant, long a fisherman to his trade, now retired. After
that first visit, he made many others, always bringing a gift. It might
be mackerel that he had fished from the bay at five in the morning, or
some spider-crabs that his wife had cooked, or a basket of oysters, or
a lobster . . . He'd tell me (at the second visit, he did come into the
house) that there was less and less fish in the bay waters, because men
anxious to pay their debts on boats that had cost them from a
hundred million to three hundred million francs would set out huge
stretches of net and 'If you eat your soup with a ladle, it doesn't last
long.' The pleasure yachts also took their toll. As to the oysters, he'd
laid out a park with some mates, and they were doing well, despite
the occasional illness and the sargasso weed in the bay . . .
  He was a talker, Roparz, and he'd go fast from one subject to
another, but I gradually got together the facts of his life, well, some of
them, the main lines. At the end of the 1930s, he was at St Malo,
where he wrote what he called his 'thesis' on ocean currents. Then
hardly out of sea-school, he'd taken part in an expedition to the
Kerguelen archipelago, in particular to the islands of Saint-Paul and
Amsterdam, which had been a disaster: three months stranded there,
in a desolate landscape of volcanic rock surrounded by rough seas,
the home of petrels, penguins, terns and skuas, and the old haunt of
sealers from Nantes, Le Havre and New Bedford. By the late 1940s,
he was a 'fish boss' on the Newfoundland run. Ten years later, he was
in Africa, fishing along the coasts of Senegal, Guinea and the Ivory

Coast, and at some time in between he was fishing lobsters off Tabarka. Then he gave up the ocean-going fishing and came home. He bought a trawler and fished in the Bay of Lannion, that had lain dormant for years, and over by the Triagoz. But one day he'd lent the boat to a friend, and it had been wrecked, with all hands lost. He hadn't started up again. He had a small boat now, with a Lister engine, and worked the bay for pollack, bream, mackerel, gilthead, dogfish and gurnard. Lannion Bay used to be full of sardines, but they'd moved away about 1950 (maybe a change in the Gulf Stream?). He had a Japanese net, close-meshed, invisible in the water, and with that, in two hours, the fishing was done. Before, with ordinary nets, you had to leave them down twelve hours, and the fish would be eaten in part by conger eels and crabs. He was all alone in the bay from 1961 to 1967, then others got into the act.

It was from Roparz I got my first rudiments of Breton. That's how I came to learn that Côtes-du-Nord was Aodou an Hanternoz and that the Ivory Coast was Aod an Olifant. Other words for north were *kreiznoz, sterenn, norzh* and *nord*. 'Learn to keep your head' in Breton is *'arabat koll an nord'*. The big ocean out there is *Mor Atlantel*, though in more intimate terms, referring to its more immediate precincts, it's *Mor Kelt* or *Mor Sterenn*. To indicate that the sea's getting rough, you say: *'Ar mor a ya droug ennañ.'* As for sea-birds, they are *evned-mor* or *laboused-mor* Roparz also wrote in Breton: poems and short stories. He'd always wanted to write, but first there had been the fishing, to earn a living, and then there'd been the family, and it was only now that he was retired (though still president of the local branch of the *Crédit Maritime*) that he found a little time. He'd recount to me the stories he published in the local newpapers: the one, for example, about a certain Tomaz Bihan, who fell in love with a *girlenn* ('a pretty girl'), a *sukenn* ('a sweet one'), and who went to see her father: 'I'd like to borrow your punt to cross the river.' – 'But you've already got a punt!' – 'No, I mean the other punt.' What he was divulging to me there, he'd say, were 'the secret ways of our Brittany': you never broached a subject directly, you always went round about it. In fact, his style was like that: he'd spin out his thread like a spider, spin it out, spin it out, then bingo, he'd make his catch. He'd tell me about the manuscript he'd got together and that he was going to put forward for the Prix Xavier de l'Anglois – 'You might say it's the Breton Goncourt', he'd say (and I'd inwardly groan) – and about the trouble he was having with a priest on the jury who was out to sink him for his grammar. And he'd go on about the literary programmes he listened to on radio and TV: 'They keep me up to date.' I much preferred to hear Roparz talking about fishing than about literature, but I'd listen to him – it was only when he got on to those literary programmes that I felt like stopping him. Desperately, I'd try to get him off the literary opinions of Petiton or Lardon and on to more interesting topics. Sometimes I'd succeed. One day, in the middle of his telling me about some novel, I managed to deflect his attention to an old compass I'd brought back from Japan. He told me it was a *compas liquide*, or *compas humide* – using water, with alcohol, so it wouldn't freeze. And went on to other types of compass: for example, the *pointe sèche*, which tended to move about too much. Nowadays, to indicate directions they just use numbers: *Faites cap sur le* 280 ('280 steady as you go'). But the old language was more poetic: '*Nordé, noroît, nordé quart nord, su-ouet, suroît* . . .'

Roparz died three years ago, from what in Breton is called *krign beo* ('the gnawer-at-life'), in other words, cancer. I've just gone down to the library to look at some of his books in Breton. In a book of his short stories, *En ur ruilhañ bili* ('Pebbles rolling on the beach'), I find this dedication: 'To Kenneth White, my Scottish cousin, so that, some day, he'll roll the pebbles of Breton on the shore of his tongue.'

Kenavo, Roparz.

It was a rainy morning in early September. A big van drew up at the gate, and out of it stepped a well-built handsome fellow about thirty-five years old, with thinning hair and a large copper ring in his left ear. He told me that he was a contorsionist and equilibrist, and that he travelled the roads 'from Brest to Budapest', sometimes doing galas, sometimes working on his own, '*à la manche*'. He travelled a lot at one time with the gypsies – Manouches mostly, but sometimes Yeniches or Sinti. It wasn't easy for a *gajo* (a foreigner, a sedentary fellow) to join the gypsies, but once in, if they took to you, you were 'an accepted man'. He'd even become friends with the *kakou*, the medicine-man of one group. Among the gypsies, he said, people who did circus work called themselves 'circassians'. He then tells me about his van, the inside of which he rigged up himself. He even has a 'visitors' room' in it. He knows people all over Europe with whom he can get a shake-down, and he shared at one time in Paris lodging space with artists in the old cold-storage buildings of the Austerlitz railway station. Nowadays in Paris, he parks in a quiet little alley in the 11th district, but now and then, though, he'll park right plunk on the Place de la Concorde, and invite people for dinner. He had a dog for six years: Lovelito, she was called. When he felt depressed, he used to sleep with her. But Lovelito had been run over by a car in Paris. He told me he was following a teaching: some kind of Buddhist–Christian syncretism, ultimately stemming from the man (an Indian or Tibetan sage) who'd given the otherworld messages to Madame Blavatsky. He'd already gone through the first two stages, and expected a lot from the third. He said he had healing faculties himself, a question of energy, animals feel it. To wind up his visit (he says he'd been meaning to pay me a visit for years – almost did, in Pau), he did a complicated contorsion on the floor of the library. I then accompanied him to his van and saw him off with a wave on the road.

The chap who turned up today is just back from the Marquesas, and is about to leave for Turkey and India. He worked for a while in a pharmaceutical firm (commercial section) in Paris, put a little money aside, then left the job to move around. He calls himself 'a searcher'.

Went through what he calls a symbolic suicide ('death of the ego') a few years back. Is now on the tracks of the Alun people, but mainly in search of his own possibilities. He takes from a folder a little cardboard kind of mandala he's worked out: a sheet of concentric circles, coloured, that fits into another sheet of concentric circles, with a white centre. Whip that sheet away, and you have a sheet of white paper, with no centre. That's your 'white world', he says. He leaves me with a compact disc, and the machine to play it – he'll pick it up again in six months, or a year, or whenever. The disc is by a German group, Tangerine Dream, and has pieces on it such as 'No man's land'. When I ask this chap his name, he says: 'Just call me Max.' He's a Breton, his folks farmer people from Pontivy.

This was a printer-publisher from New Hampshire, New England, USA. He'd asked if I might have something for him to print in a luxury edition and since he was going to be in Europe for a month, maybe he could come visit me for a day? I said OK. It was maybe a time of low resistance; I was just out of a bout of flu. And then I always have at the back of my mind the idea that, whatever happens, *something* good can come of it. When this dapper little fellow in the beribboned soft hat, with the steel-rim glasses, got off the train at Lannion, he told us in a querulous tone he had a headache because he hadn't had any coffee that morning. He'd been afraid to miss the train and had left his Paris hotel without. I said he could have got some on the train, but he said he hadn't wanted to risk leaving his seat. The first thing then was to get his sore head a dose of coffee. We'd arranged to go to a restaurant, so there we went, and I asked for a pot of coffee before the meal . . . OK, so you know about the coffee. But wait till you hear about the wisdom teeth. This guy had had big trouble with his wisdom teeth, in fact he'd had an infection. I spare you the details – but he didn't spare me. 'Oh dear, I'm sure I'm boring you with all this,' he said at one point. I didn't say anything. After the wisdom teeth, he went on to tell me about the amoebas he'd caught down in Merida 'Oh dear,' he said, in conclusion. I mean, conclusion to that part. Because all this was just by way of introduction. Now he got on to literature. Had I read *The Mosquito Net* by Henry B. Stanford? I said no. He proceeded to tell me about it. It's about this man who's afraid of a nuclear war, and he goes down to Central America where he rigs up a machine to make ice which he sells to the natives. He gets killed at the end, by the natives, with a vulture picking out his eyes. 'And they put him on his own ice,' I say, just to show I'm participating. 'Oh no', he says, 'that would be a cliché, wouldn't it?' 'No doubt.' By this time, we've finished the meal, and I'm getting desperate, I'm going to have this boyo on my hands for *two whole days* (yes, during the meal he told me his schedule meant he'd leave not the next day, but the next again).

Out of the restaurant, as we passed along the Quai d'Aiguillon, he said: 'So this is the main drag', and when he saw a red light, he snickered: 'the red light district, huh?' At that moment, a bus passed with some navy men in uniform in it: 'Is that the French navy?', he said, looking very interested.

Later that night he told me about his home in New Hampshire, and about the cycle of the year, which begins with the running of the maple syrup in February. There, I had a flicker of interest, which was rapidly extinguished when he started to tell me about his neighbours, Clarence and Betty, with whom he sometimes played Monopoly. He meets people only once a week when he goes to the supermarket in the neighbouring town. The rest of the time he listens to opera. It was one day when he had toothache and he was fiddling with the knobs of the radio, and there was Verdi. Without the art of opera, life would be absolutely unbearable. He comes to Europe as often as he can, because his literary contacts are all there. He knows a man in Luxemburg: Humphrey Davenport. That name mean anything to me? No? His uncle was Ronald Gribble, the writer, who knew everybody in the literary world of the 1970s. Guy is in banking. Or was. But he lost his job. His wife, who is a Habsburg, is going to become a secretary . . . Our man had lived for a while in Oxford-shire, at Impington, as a guest of the poetess Cecily Wobley-Wobley, who was related to Charles Darwin and who was a friend of Count Stephen Belowski. Did I know her work? I said no. Did I know Jennifer Beerbohm, the poetess, who was related to Benjamin Disraeli (maybe I'm getting the genealogy all mixed up)? I said I didn't. Her father was an actor, he said, and began to tell me about the plays he had written. 'Two days', I'm saying to myself, 'two whole fuckin' wasted days!'

But they finally went by. On the morning of his departure, at breakfast, our guest from America asked me if we had any mice. He'd had a lot of trouble with those sassy little varmints in New Hamp-shire, till he found a new type of trap in the local hardware store, the one run by Dave and Marjorie, who have two very nice daughters, one of them, Madge, had a truly mortifying experience at a school-leaving party, it was crashed by a bunch of beer-drinkers, the police raided them, and her name was in the newspaper, that's all right for Massachusetts, not for New Hampshire – oh, but, yes, dear dear, he was talking abut the mouse-traps. A new invention made in USA, no messy blood, the mechanism snaps and the mice are stifled. If I invited him back, he would, he declared, bring me two, as a gift. I said thanks, it was a nice thought.

A long white Plymouth pulled up at the gate. Out of it stepped a man in a colonial helmet, wearing square-toed blanco'd shoes, beside him a neat little Japanese-looking girl about fifteen years old. Aha, says I to myself, what have we here?

He was a Breton, born in a little village here on the north coast. That was in the early 1930s. At the time of the war, he was on the Normandy coast. After the war, he joined the French airforce, and by the mid-1950s, as a member of the 1ère *escouade de chasse*, he was one of the early breakers of the sound barrier: in an F84F Thunderstreak, at 1240 kilometres an hour. That sound-breaking, he told me, had begun with Neville Duke, in a Spitfire: 'He'd been zooming about when suddenly the plane flipped and he found himself in a terrible tailspin, spiralling like mad.' Back at the base, Duke had talked of the strange thing that had occurred: 'Something really weird happens. I was in a death-dive . . . at 475 miles an hour . . .' That was the start of the studies on MAC, and of a whole series of *macbusters*, of which my visitor had been among the first fifty. But now it wasn't planes that interested him, he said, it was books. 'Sound-breaking literature, as I see it, began with Nietzsche,' I said. And we were at it for three hours . . .

The fifteen-year-old girl was his daughter, he told me.

One day, a young Welshman turned up – a student of French and Russian at Cambridge. He had been in Brittany for a few months, teaching English at the college in Lannion, improving his French, and learning a little Breton into the bargain. A year before he'd been in Leningrad (clammy climate, millions of mosquitoes, town built on a swamp), where he'd lived with other foreign students in a building opposite the old Imperial Palace that had once been a brothel. He knows all the bars between Lannion and Le Vieux Marché and gets drunk regularly: not only is that an aid to fraternisation, he says, it's good for phonetics.

It was a wet morning, early June, about half past eight. I was sitting with Catou on my knees, talking with Marie-Claude, when I saw a chap coming to the door. About thirty years old, ill-shaven. Shit. 'I just wanted to pay you a little visit and I've got my breakfast ready in the car, can I have it here?' I say I've a lot on my hands, but that I'll be pleased (thanks to the education my mother gave me, I'm really a very polite guy) to have a little talk with him. We go over to the study. He's from the Finistère, lives in the Monts d'Arrée with his 75-year-old mother, goes for a little trip now and then, likes moving around this part of the country, thinks it's like a garden. I ask him how he lives, what he lives on. 'I compose poetry.' OK, but how did he manage economically? 'Oh, I make out', he says. Meaning what? 'Oh, things you can't talk about too openly – tricks of the trade.' I say he's beating about the bush. It comes out that he has the RMI (minimal insertion allowance), plus a handicapped allowance, all in all about 3,400 F a month. 'You don't look handicapped,' I say. 'Not really,' he says'. But he explains that when he was young, he was very nervous, and, he went on, giving me to understand he'd woodwinked a psychiatrist, 'when you've read Lacan and Freud a bit . . .' I ask him what had brought him to me. 'Oh, I've read your books and I'd like to have them all. I'd like to buy one now, this morning.' I tell him I don't have them around for sale, but there's a bookshop in Lannion. He doesn't look too interested in that. 'What's your name,' I say. 'Gwendal'. 'Well, Gwendal, thanks for the visit, I've got to get down to work now.' 'It's true, everybody knows you're a tremendous worker.' I stand up and go to the door. 'What about my breakfast?' he says. I say he can take it in the country. 'In the rain?' he says. 'Why not?', I say, 'I've done that often enough, and anyway you've got your car.' 'Easy enough to see where you came from,' he says, meaning no doubt the stormy wilds of Scotland. 'Anyway I'm glad to have met you.' 'Me too, Gwendal, I'll be seeing you.'

The young chap who came to visit me today opened, two years ago, a little restaurant in Tréguier. At the beginning, it was a total disaster. Especially when he found out that the waitress who'd seemed so perfect was helping herself in the cash-drawer. But now it was running OK. He'd just bought 700 kilos of vegetaline, which meant he had confidence in the future. But living conditions weren't too good. He lived with his wife and two kids in the house of his parents. Now and then he felt the need to get away. He usually went to Ushant, he said, where he'd read books, walk on the shore, and not talk for days on end. That helped him to live. This time he had decided to come and visit me.

It was a rainy afternoon, late June, about half past twelve. The postman had just come by, and I was going through the mail when I heard the gate opening and somebody crunching along the gravel of the courtyard.

There he was ringing the bell.

'I've come from Quimper. I won't waste your time. I've brought you a manuscript.'

He was maybe in his late twenties, tall and spare, with close-cropped reddish hair, his whole manner rather stiff. I said to come in and sit down.

He told me he wrote poetry, had been writing it since he was eleven years of age.

'That was young,' I said.

'Yes, indeed,' he said.

The manuscript he now handed over to me in a business-like kind of way, a bulky yellow folder, had been completed, he informed me, two years before and had taken him eight years to write. He'd already sent it to 'the biggest publishers' in Paris and it had always been refused. He had been to see Yves-Donatien Hallégouët, the Parisian novelist of Breton origins who sometimes lived at his family manor near Morlaix, who had told him three things: that he received through the post ten manuscripts a week, which he threw directly into the dustbin, because he had no time to waste on rubbish; that nobody read poetry any more; and that the best possible thing he could do would be to commit suicide.

'Straight from the shoulder,' I said.

'Yes, indeed,' he said.

He'd then gone to see Paul Soulier, a Parisian writer not of Breton origins, who worked at a publishing firm. He'd gone to the offices of the firm, asked to see Soulier, and was told he wasn't in. But our man, beginning to get wise, didn't believe this at all. So he waited outside the door till closing-time, waylaid Soulier, and shoved the manuscript into his arms. It was returned to him six months later, with a little note from the said Soulier saying he was a specialist of novels, no judge of poetry, and that our man should write a novel – if it was a best-seller, he might get his poetry published then. So many people had told our friend the same thing that he had in fact begun to write a novel: a love story tied in with the Resistance movement in the Alps. 'A surefire thing,' I said. 'With that, you're bound to make it.' But it was poetry, he said, that interested him. Wasn't poetry the supreme form of art?

While he was speaking, I'd opened the bulky yellow folder, had seen his name and glanced at some of the pages:

'Monsieur Flanchec,' I said, but got no farther, because he interrupted me sharply.

'Maëlstrom,' he said.

'What's that?'

'Hugo Maëlstrom – that's my poet's name.'

'That's quite a name, isn't it ?'

He told me he'd always admired Victor Hugo, and had always been attracted to the sound of the word 'maëlstrom'.

'Well, then Mr Maëlstrom,' I said, 'I'm afraid I can't help you a great deal. You know I'm not a publisher, nor a professional reader for a publisher, and I don't have any time to spare – look, come over to my workshop a minute.'

I took him over the workshop and showed him the cardboard boxes full of manuscripts I also received through the post.

'You see the position?' I said.

'Yes, indeed,' he said.

But wasn't it terrible that nobody could help him? It wasn't only Victor Hugo he admired. He also liked Arthur Rimbaud and René Char and Kenneth White. And, what's more, he'd worked out the problem of the mute 'e'.

'The what?,' I said.

'The mute e,' he said.

He then told me that the mute 'e' was *the* big question in French prosody, after the alexandrine. Nobody had solved it. Not even the free-verse people, not even the Surrealists. He had.

I felt like a change of conversation.

'Mr Flanchec,' I said.

'Maëlstrom,' he said.

'Mr Maëlstrom, I could say, leave me your manuscript. But you'd write me back in two or six weeks, and I still might not have read it.'

'I'm in no hurry,' he said. 'Poetry is never in a hurry.'

'That's just what I was going to say. Yourself and time – they are your two best critics.'

'But it's not criticism I want, it's publishing.'

'Why not try smaller publishers?'

'When I see the poor work they put out, I'm disgusted. I won first prize in a poetry competition open to all Normandy when I was seventeen.'

'How about trying a poem or two in magazines?'

'No, no, this is a book,' he said, pointing to the bulky yellow folder, 'it is a unity of three hundred pages. I don't want to pick out a poem here and there. A book of poems should be a unity. That's what Charles Baudelaire said.'

I said I could sympathise with that. But even Baudelaire had published a poem or two here and there in reviews . . . Anyway, all I could do was wish him luck.

'Well, at least you were willing to talk to me, and you didn't tell me to shoot myself, like the other one.'

'How do you make a living, Mr Maëlstrom?'

'I give lessons.'

'In a school?'

'Oh no, private lessons.'

'On what?'

'Mathematics, physics, chemistry.'

He'd taught first in Le Havre, his home town, then in Rouen, and now he was in Brest. A lot of people wanted lessons there; the Bretons were eager to learn.

'Best of luck,' I said again.

I liked him. But what can you do?

This afternoon, late August, a young fellow of about twenty turned up at the gate. 'I'm not disturbing you?' 'No, no, in you come.' (What else can you say once it's happened?) He was a student from Angers, and was just back from doing the trip I'd done years ago along the north bank of the St Lawrence. He'd also been to the Ardèche, to visit Gourgounel, the old farm-house I used to have there. I make a pot of tea, and we sit out on the grass. He tells me what sparked off everything for him was the reading of a poem, 'The absolute body', in *Handbook for the Diamond Country*. He was in bed one night when he read it. 'It emptied me out. Turned the world upside down. The sensation lasted a few minutes. If I'd been standing up, I'd have fallen.' This was a welcome change from the mute 'e'.

It was an afternoon in September, and I was sauntering around the garden. I saw a burly fellow in a tracksuit going by on the road. He passed our gate and disappeared out of sight. A few seconds later I heard a shout. It was the same man, now standing at the gate, and beckoning to me in an impatient way to come over. His manner was so peremptory I stayed where I was, saying simply: 'Can I be of any help to you, Monsieur?' He gave me another authoritative sign. 'What do you want?' I asked. This time he spoke: 'Are you the owner of this house?' 'Yes,' I replied. He said he'd like to speak to me. I now left the apple-tree where I was standing and went up to the gate.

'I want to have a word with you.' The tone was aggressive and threatening.

'You do? Go ahead.'

'You are English?'

'Scottish.'

'Naturalised French,' he says, with a nasty little laugh, then, seeing I don't look too pleased with his banter, he adds:

'I was just joking.'

'What brings you here?'

'I heard of you. You're a writer, aren't you?'

'That's right.'

'A specialist?'

'What do you mean by that?'

'You do nothing else?'

'I do several things. But it all turns around the one.'

'Well, I'm a gendarme, retired, and I want to write a book.'

Now closer to his face, I noted the bristling grey-white moustache, the gold tooth, and the very pale-blue eyes.

'I have no instruction. I left school at thirteen, in 1942. The year 1942 – does that mean anything to you? I saw the enemy on the soil of my country. I wanted to join the army. They told me I was too young. But I've always wanted to fight. When I was a lad, I did Breton wrestling. Do you know about Breton wrestling? I had forty fights: thirty-eight victories, one draw, one surprise attack. I got into the army. They'd say to us: "There's a machine-gun nest over there, with seven fellows in it – shut them up." There were three of us, we did the job. With knives. That's the way it was. I've always said, what another man can do, I can do. I was demobilised from the army, and I went into the gendarmerie. I know a thing or two, and I've always spoken the truth. I've got it all down in my book. It's the story of a dead man, a suicide. There are lots of suicides in the gendarmerie. They keep an eye on me. I've been photographed ten times. They know where I am, all the time. They know where I am, right this moment. You didn't expect that, did you? I've received 144 anonymous letters in fifteen months, threatening my life. Five years ago, I was called up before a board of psychiatrists. "We're here to ascertain if you're mad or not," they said. I didn't lose my temper, I kept my head. I know there was a fellow behind the door ready to jump in and give me a jag.

I know how they work; I know the ropes. "Mr Bocquého," they said, "we know you're not mad, but just don't tell the truth all the time." The week after, they called in my wife. "Madame Bocquého," they said, "are you aware that your husband is congenitally insane?" But my wife was a match for them; she was up to their tricks. "Was he mad when he was sent to Indochina?" she said. "Was he mad when they sent him to Algeria? Does the army employ mad folk?" Oh, she has a tongue in her head, that woman, and she knows how to use it.'

'And have they left you alone since then?' I asked.

'No, no, I'm telling you – I've been sent 144 anonymous letters in fifteen months. I had the captain of gendarmerie dismissed from the sector. I was coming out of my house when I noticed a car. A police car. So I said to myself: Will I make off to the right or to the left? I jouked off to the left. But there was another police car waiting for me there. And there was a third one farther on. I sent in a complaint to the chief magistrate. I told him that the captain of gendarmerie was using fascist methods. A fortnight later, I saw in the paper that captain had been transferred. I can't say it's because of me, but it's some coincidence . . . I showed my book to a schoolteacher. He showed me the method to follow. I did it all on my own. I'm no stupider than the next man. I've got a daughter who's leaving soon for Japan as an interpreter. Yes, sir. A journalist has had a look at it. He served ten years in the navy, and he sees things the same way as I do. I wondered if you'd like to come in on it too?'

I had a better feeling of the man now than I'd had at the beginning, when he'd been all sly looks and sneers. But I told him I had an awful lot of work on hand myself and that I was sure he'd make out, with the help of his friends, the schoolteacher and the journalist.

'Well, *kenavo*,' he said.

'*Kenavo*.'

Two students in communication at Rennes drop by. The girl, Muriel, also does studies in Celtic, the boy, Bernard, in Chinese (started

Chinese because of me, he says). They've just been to the Seven Islands bird reserve, and have an idea of a programme for the radio. Want to give it 'another dimension'. I talk into their tape recorder for an hour or so, about gannets and Nietzsche and Li Po.

One morning a guy turned up in a pink tracksuit with a red rucksack on his back. Maybe twenty-five years old. Lives in the southern suburbs of Paris, and earns his living accompanying groups of schoolkids on their two weeks a year of mountain or shore. He's on the books of an agency, the conditions being 160 F a day, with board and lodging, and one day off a week with some free time every day. Quite recently, he didn't know why, there in the south suburbs, he started writing poems: 'poems about revolt and nature'. Everytime he felt 'the jiminy cricket' in his head, he wrote a poem. Now he was actually out on the coast, though, it wasn't the same trip. He found himself writing love poems. He wanted to leave me a jotterful of his efforts, but was particularly keen to know with what agency or office he should register them, so nobody would steal his ideas. I told him I hadn't a clue, but that in any case there was probably no great danger. He said maybe not, but he'd been writing for three months now and it was time he got a book published. I suggested he could wait just a bit longer.

An afternoon in May, and a visit from Jacqueline Lebrun, painter. Did her art studies in Strasbourg and Paris. Shows me a series of paintings: landscapes and seascapes. One of the landscapes has a strange dance of flames, and I say it reminds me of something Tibetan. She tells me she has travelled in the East, was fascinated in her childhood by Marco Polo's travels and the Silk Road, and meditation kiosques. She then goes on to ikons, telling me about the bottom layer, red, of those in Novgorod . . . As I accompany Jacqueline back to the gate, we pass the door of the old building, which is a strange, 'ogival' shape for a farm building: the stones may have been lifted from a chapel

somewhere. When I say *porte ogivale*, Jacqueline corrects me: it would
be better to say *arc brisé* or *tiers point*.

About half past one, a clear day in late May, I saw him standing at the
gate: a young fellow, tall, long-haired, with espadrilles on his feet,
tied with string around the ankles. 'Are you Kenneth White?' he said.
I said: 'Yes, that's me.' 'I've come to see you.' 'OK, let's go into the
library.' He was from near Alençon, in Normandy. Name: Jean-
Michel. Had done music studies in Paris, thereafter, at a more
advanced level, in Lyons. Classic guitar, and composition. Then
two years ago he had given up music, wanting to write. He'd written a
long poem on the Ys legend ('It gave me a basis'), then one on the
Tajmahal, then one called 'Dazibao'. Then, a year ago he'd come
across my books: 'I've studied your books. That set me reforming
myself, and working with new formulas. I decided I'd undertake a
long work in depth.' He went to Ushant, read a lot of books in
science and in philosophy while rereading mine, moved around a lot
out of doors, and wrote only haiku. Then he started into a long poem
on Ushant. It was still, he said, a bit sickly and weepy, it was still 'me
and my problems', still heavy 'with the weight I've been dragging
about with me for years', but maybe there were signs in it of
something else. He'd like me to read it. In fact, he'd like me to
be interested in him. He'd like to have a permanent dialogue with me,
now he was starting out on his 'blue road'. He and his girlfriend had
set out from his parents' home in Normandy about a week before,
with the intention of walking all the way to Gwenved. They'd take a
month to do it, and he'd write a kind of notebook all the time, that
would be a present for me, and also maybe a kind of visiting card.
That was the plan. But once outside the little roads of the Orne, they
met up with a lot of stinking, noisy traffic, which made walking
difficult. Nevertheless they'd done seven hours a day of it for a week,
but he found he was too tired at night to write a line. So they'd
decided to take the train at Laval and had arrived in Lannion that

morning. I asked him if he intended to stick around the Trébeurden area for a while. He said he'd come to see me, that's all. I told him I was deep in work, didn't want to break the rhythm. Maybe he could leave me his manuscript, and we could meet, say, in three days' time, at eleven o'clock? That was fine, he answered, he'd got a tent, could I suggest a good place to camp? I said, why not Île-Grande, and he and his girlfriend could have a look at the Bird Centre while they were at it. On the Monday, I learned that they'd never gone the length of Île-Grande. On their way down the Goaslagorn valley, they'd seen an old house – it was closed, but there was a shelter for goats and they'd shacked up there. I read through his Ushant poem, full of 'Buddha buoys' and 'sardine clouds' and with phrases like this: 'I'm still a numbskull, but it won't be for long.' When we met again after the three days, before even I had time to say what I thought of it, he insisted I must realise it was only a beginning, that his 'blue road' was only starting; he just wanted to know if there was a sign or two in it. I said sure, sure, there was. What he wanted to do now was go to the Molène archipelago, where there were a lot of dolphins and grey seals and puffins. He'd tried before to get on to one of the islands for a stay, but the Bird Protection people wouldn't let him. But he'd just written them a letter – 'I used your vocabulary' – and he hoped that would do the trick.

I said I hoped it would.

He was a mathematician. Attached to the CNRS (National Centre for Scientific Research). Started off in practical physics, then moved to theoretical physics, and finally to mathematics. He had a thesis in physics behind him, and had just finished a thesis on mathematics – in very abstract areas, he said, where mathematics becomes aesthetics. He told me there are three principal schools of mathematics: the Russian school, the French school and the American school. He'd just sent in an article, in English, to the *Annals of Mathematics* at Princeton, one of the toughest of maths reviews. He hoped his

English was a little better than the very queer French some of the Japanese mathematicians wrote in. A few years ago, he had a nervous breakdown and moved from Paris to Brittany. He'd loved the place, lived there for a year, before going back to the big city. But he'd found Paris both hectic and small-minded. Came back to the coast, living in an austere kind of luxury, practising Zen, interested, in his own way, in the Chinese *Book of Changes*. He'd had to leave the house he'd rented, and was now in another one. Approaching it, he'd seen a goat browsing, and he'd taken that as a good sign: Capricorn-Saturn, the star of solitude and great realisation. Coming to Gwenved this afternoon, he'd felt he'd been there before. There are places and events like that, he said, no simple equation can explain them.

Echoes of Scotland

Rain was battering at the window of the restaurant, but through it, *blink-blink-blink*, you could see the Triagoz lighthouse. There had been five of us at table, and now the *patronne* had joined us, bringing with her a bottle of vodka, though, horrible to relate, she said her favourite drink was whisky and coca-cola, mixed.

The evening was Yvonne's idea, Yvonne Ledanois, who had a post in Interceltic Relations at the *Maison de la Culture* in Rennes. Donald Donaldson, of the School of Scottish Studies in Edinburgh, had dropped in to see her at her home in Guingamp, and, since he wanted to stay a few days in Brittany, she had sent him to a hotel run by a cousin of hers at Trestel, near Port-Blanc. Yvonne phoned me up on the Sunday suggesting a meeting with Donald on the Monday night, so Marie-Claude and I drove over on what was a grey drizzling evening in August.

Donald Donaldson turned out to be about seven feet tall, ruddy-faced, with four strands of very white hair on a shining skull, the foremost of those strands continually falling over his brow. He looked a bit like a retired major of the British army – till he'd give one of his great gumsy laughs (he has not a tooth left in his gub), when he looked like a hilarious demon. A habit of his when he was speaking was to make a gesture over his heart with his right hand, as if to suggest that all he was saying was straight out of that ilk.

Donald began by telling me that he was born in Perthshire, of a Piskie family:

'A *what* family?'

'A Piskie family.'

'What's that?' says I, thinking vaguely of intoxicated fairies.

'Piskie, Episcopalian.'

I'd been so long away from the niceties of Scottish theology that I'd forgotten the existence of that dying but adamant remnant. The dialectics of theology in Scotland is usually confined, as in Ireland, to a murky and violent debate between Proddie Dogs and Dirty Papes, but behind that frontline, vulgar and footballish skirmish you have innumerable more subtle ones, involving weird ethno-theological tribes such as Wee Frees, Glasgow Galatians, Dundonian Shakers, Aberdonian Apocalyptics and Pitskelly Piskies. As Piskies, Donald's family whole-heartedly hated Presbyterians, a mean-minded psychologically edgy lot, according to their estimations, who had done immeasurable damage to Scotland. The way his mother put it ('She was a very outspoken woman,' said Donald), those Presbyterian buggers 'wouldny gi ye the steam aff their shite'. While he was on his mother, he said she could fairly sing songs, in Gaelic, like 'An aitearachd àrd', about the high swelling of the sea, and the sound of it, the sound of waves over sand. 'My mother, my God,' said Donald, 'she could sing that song. She could put any one to shame when she sang that song', and he sang a bit of it himself, so we could appreciate the assonances:

> An ataireachd àrd bhuan
> Cluinn fuaim na hataireachd àrd
> Tha torunn a' chuain
> Mar chualas leam-s'e nam phàisd . . .

'The eternal swell, listen to the high swelling of the sea. It's the thunder of the waves as I heard it when I was a bairn. Without change, without respite, swirling around the sands of the shore. The eternal swell, listen to the sound of the sea's high swelling.'

Donald was educated in Perthshire, learning Latin and Greek, and then a Jewish teacher in his school had said that Scottish poetry was fine, but that nothing could beat Dante and he should learn Italian. So he did. After that early Scottish school, he went to an English school, because his mother had gone down to London in search of work, and then he went up to Cambridge, where he studied Modern Languages, Italian in particular:

> D'in su la vetta della torre antica,
> Passero solitario, alla campagna
> Cantando vai finchè non more il giorno;
> Ed erra l'armonia per questa valle

he quoted, from Leopardi's 'Il Passero Solitario'.

When the war broke out, Donald served in Italy, where he learned more Italian, and then in Libya, where he learned Arabic:

saqatni bumaiya l-bubbi rabatu muqlati
waka'si mubaiya man 'ani l-busni jallati

– that's *tawil* metre from a poem by Ibn al-Farid, twelfth-century Cairo, he told me.

After the war, he went back to Cambridge, completed his degree, and started writing. Thereafter, he went back to Italy, and did some work for the great Italian song-collector, Caltino. In fact, it was his, Donald's voice, singing Italian songs, that Caltino recorded in Milan. Most of the Italian song-collectors and folklorists, said Donald, were men of the study who didn't much like humping about mountain villages unless there was a good hotel with a decent restaurant in the vicinity. Whereas doing without a good hotel and a decent restaurant, and trekking about mountains, that, he said, was second nature to a Scotsman.

When he came back to Scotland, Donald was convinced that there must be a great folk-singer somewhere in the land, a woman ('it's a female tradition'), and he set out to find her. He went up to Aberdeenshire, and started hunting about the countryside, but no luck. Then somebody said he should try in the city of Aberdeen itself, because there was a woman there who sang the old songs. When he turned up at the market where he'd been told he would be likely to find her, she'd just gone home. He went after her.

'I chapped at the door: *knock, knock, knock.*'

Donald, who has a good sense of story-telling, actually knocks on the table.

'And she came to the door. And I said: Are you Jeannie Robertson? And when she said, ay, it was her, I started singing a song. It was ''The Back o' Bennachie'':

> *As I cam' roun' by Bennachie*
> *A bonnie young lassie there I did see*

> *I gied her a wink and she smiled at me*
> *At the back o' Bennachie*

and when I'd finished a verse or two, she said: Come in now, and I'll show you how that song *should* be sung.'

So, that's how Donald met and discovered Jeannie Robertson, who was thereafter to become celebrated as a folk-singer all over Scotland. 'I discovered Jeannie Robertson, it was me that discovered Jeannie Robertson', he says, with a gumsy laugh, putting his right hand ritually over his heart.

Donald did a lot of story-collecting too, among the tinkers of the north-east, for example: the metal-workers who'd taken to the roads, still making a living up there mending pots and pans, and rounding out their income from that by fishing for pearls from mussels in the Helmsdale and Oykil rivers. He remembered one time in particular. The tinker band they'd got in touch with on the heather were a bit wary of Donald's crowd – 'afraid that we were Burkers'. It was not so long ago in the memory of the tinkers that they, like other vagrants, would be killed and their corpses sent to the hospitals and universities as surgical material – a trade which Burke and his accomplice Hare had plied with such great profit in Edinburgh in the early nineteenth century. But gradually confidence was won, and they told him about an old man called Blind Alec. Donald went to see him:

'Do you have any stories?' (*A bheil sgeulachdan agaibh?*)

'Oh, yes, I have many stories.' (*O, tha. Tha iomadh sgeulachd agam.*)

'Do you have any stories about Ossian?' (*A bheil sgeulachdan agaibh mu Oisean?*)

'I have many a story about Ossian.' (*Tha iomadh sgeulachd mu Oisean.*)

And the man told him stories about Ossian and the Fianna for hours on end.

'Ach,' says Donald, 'it is a pity that a poet like you doesn't have the Gaelic. You could make fabulous use of it.'

'You know,' says I, 'there was a time I went about in Glasgow with a wee grass-green book in my pocket, and it was MacLaren's Gaelic grammar. But I soon began to feel there were other and more pressing things to be done.'

'Ah well,' said Donald, and proceeded to tell me a story about Boswell and Johnson, when they were on their tour in the Hebrides. They were at this big house, and this old man, this *bodach*, who was working in the garden, said to Boswell:

'Who's the big man?' (*Co am fear siod?*)

'That's the great man who created the English language.' (*S'e am fear mór a rinn a 'Bheurla.*)

'It's little the merit in that.' (*'S beag a bh'aige r'a dheanamh.*)

To round things off, Donald said he was going to sing me a song, and it was a song that should mean a lot to me, because it was a song about Cruachan of the Bens, and the Whites were MacIntyres, and that was their country. I'd always thought the Whites were Mac-Gregors, but I didn't care to argue the point. I just listened to the song:

Cruachan beann, Cruachan beann . . .

As I looked towards the window, the lights of the Triagoz lighthouse seemed a bit more blurred than they had been before.

LISTENING TO THE VOICES

Friends who have my phone number use it sparingly, preferring to let me get on with the job, and I myself tend to be very brisk and businesslike on the phone: 'OK, see you on the ninth at five o'clock, at the Café du Luxembourg' – 'Yes, you'll have the text for 18 September.' But every now and then there will be exceptions. Somebody may be going through a phase of great solitude or even depression and feel the need to chew the fat, spill the beans. So I listen in.

Boris Patrick Morvan is half Irish, half Russian, and all Breton. He can do his bit as a seaman (ask him to take a boat from Brest to Sydney, no problem) or as an aircraft pilot (he did a lot of crop-dusting in Texas, and various jobs in Africa), has been at different times in his life a mercenary, an adventurer and a flying humanitarian (Thailand and Laos, bringing out Meo refugees), and is also (but not always at the same time), an outrageous drunkard and a voracious reader of books. For months on end, even years, there will be no sign from the said Boris, and then, all of a sudden, there will be a whole spate of calls, from anywhere round the globe. This time, it's from Papeete, and he's telling me he's been there a month, and wants to scram. There are Korean trawlers cruising around (they use helicopters to spot the fish), and he hopes to get on one of them in order to make his way down to the Tonga archipelago – he has a house of bamboo on a little island there . . . He tells me that the next time he passes through Paris, he'll get a Chinaman to tattoo a phrase of one of my poems on his left arm.

Here's Plato the Greek, who arrived in Paris from Thessalonica two years ago with a wad of manuscript in his case: 'After a long trial, I am come to the mastery of kaos and I emerge the form.'

Here's Boris again, phoning this time from his home base, St Malo: Glad, as he says, to be sitting on his balcony, looking out through the pine trees at the Celtic Sea. He tells me his island plantation in Polynesia, at Tongapatu (watermelon, sweet potatoes), has been flooded in a hurricane, and his house part blown away, but he'll build it up again, some day. It had cost him a fat wad of dollars to get from Tahiti to the Tongas. In the old days, to get down to the South Pacific, he used to be able to get a berth for next to nothing on a Korean trawler out from Hawaii, making for Samoa, Pago Pago, New Zealand. But that seemed to be off nowadays. And there are no charters, only small local airline companies that cost you your eyes . . . Back in Brittany, he has the chance of a job: 'A real Britisher, a Britisher in all his glory, a perfect City type, not some phoney planter or a cunt from Kenya' wants him to take his boat, 'a fifty-fifty boat' (part sail, part motor), 'a cocktail-boat' (the guy usually used it for parties between London and Jersey) from Athens to Sidney. Only snag, the owner wants to make the trip with Boris and, for several reasons, Boris doesn't like to have owners on board: 'They can really fuck things up.' He'll probably do it, though. He'll have the boat put in good condition down at the harbour front in Athens, get together a crew of Cypriots, and sail through the Red Sea. He'll return to Tonga in December . . . 'In the meantime, don't die, you bastard. I love you like a brother!'

'Look, I know I'm a damn nuisance. But phoning you is the only way I can muster the courage to go on . . .' That's Marie-Jo talking. She'd gone down to her parents' place in Auvergne, but they obviously didn't want her around; she was anxious anyway to get back to Paris: 'I'm in the shit again, all fucked up. I made some concessions and now I'm suffering for it. After the Chinaman, there was this other guy. The serious type, works on the Stock Exchange. He said I'd have to take an Aids test – there was a time when you just did it, now you need a certificate. Anyway, it was OK. But he got scared. Says I'm too tough and that I have an Amazonian personality. Tough, an Amazon, me? Anyway, he got the wind up. And now the bastard is going out with some tart. I know he's in love with me, and I'm stuck on him, but he's just dead scared. I know all this sounds like women's magazine stuff. But there it is. I'm dead beat. After all the work I did on myself. But it always ends up shitty. One mess after the other. I've lost my room. My so-called friend threw me out, said I was too dirty. So I shacked up with a new boy. But I'm not in love with him, I don't go to bed with him, and that's getting on his nerves. And I can't go to a hotel, on account of my dog. With all that, my computer's broke down, it's got a bug or something. It's all just one shitty situation after another. I should have bumped myself off when I got back from Germany. But in Brittany I was fine, that was a good time. I've got only one dream left now: go to Tibet – walk, sleep under the stars. All the silly bitches like me are going to end up in Ladakh.'

Every now and then, I get a phonecall from Jean-Marc, who translates into French from Russian and English. At the moment, he tells me, he's translating George Orwell. Do I know of a pamphlet put out by the British Ministry of Information in April 1941? I say there are limits to my documentation. As to Orwell and *les Angliches* in general, they drive him up the wall with their lousy, drivelly, repetitive style and their lack of logic: *'leurs conneries de merde'* ('their shitty nitwittedness'). Take the 'echo phenomenon'. They all do it. Orwell for instance. He uses the word 'fashion', OK. Then three lines further on, you'll find 'in the fashion'. Repetitions to the point of inanity. *'Il se branle les couilles pendant cinquante ans.'* ('He wanks himself for half a century.') Here and there, you come across something that's faintly interesting, but before it gets developed, there they go into their 'good, bad' rigmarole again. *'Des* good, bad *qui se balladent partout! Ça me sèche complètement la guette!'* ('Goods and bads staggering about all over the place. It's enough to drive you bonkers.') If he wasn't getting paid pretty well to translate this tripe, he'd drop it.

Boris of St Malo is phoning from Oslo. He's been climbing in Norway with a Czech friend, an ex-Anapurna guide. At one point they were completely lost, at 9000 feet, in a terrible snowstorm. But, he says, he had a bottle of chianti with him and one of my books. They got by. Now he wants to go to Bangkok to see another friend. He'll travel by the Transsiberian, but is having trouble with visas . . . Looks as if he'll have to join a fuckin' package trip to Japan: eight days to Vladivostok and Nogoschka. He'll do that totally on vodka, of course. The idea then would be to go down the coast by boat . . . He once took a boat from Taiwan to Hong Kong. Had had the notion, 'poetically speaking', of a leisurely trip down the China coast. But there was no chance of getting into a Chinese port – he tried once, invoking damage ('My bloody mizzen fell overboard'), but he found himself surrounded by machine-gun-toting launches that pushed him back out into international waters.

Here's Federico, a Cuban who lives in the Bronx, and is fed up with it: has had enough of the violence, the insecurity, the general degradation, the post-puritan sex obsession everywhere . . . The other day, he was over in the Latin-American ghetto, where he met Theodoro, who runs a 'cosmic group' – Theodoro is his special name, given to him by superior beings he meets up with on his astral trips. He makes those astral journeys regularly, accompanied by the ghost of Che Guevara (smoking, I presume, a heavenly havana), and photographs what he sees. He has thousands of cosmic photographs. Says he has done more than the NASA with all their millions of dollars. But now he's ready to cash in himself. He wants Federico to write a book about him. Federico asks me what he should do. I suggest he might try to get out of End City.

Boris on the phone again, this time from Guernsey, sounding very sober – says he goes from one extreme to the other and has been on a dry period for a week: 'Total abstinence, yes, the in-between state, never.' He starts off talking about a six-metre cutter he had once, and that is now rotting in the harbour, St Helier, Jersey, and then gets on to the time when he was working in Laos, on 'Air Opium'. He asks me advice on books about Islam. He's going to be taking that boat through the Red Sea, after all. And he's located a little island off the coast of Kenya, may try to find himself a little Arab hut there and a dhow.

A phonecall came this evening, from Denis Jacquet. He's a good enough fellow, Denis, but chockfull of himself. He wanted to fix an appointment in Paris – OK, fine, the date's fixed, place and time, in a minute. I take it for granted he's going to put down the phone, but no, not D. J. He asks what I'm doing at the moment. My heart sinks. Oh, I say, polite as always, today I wrote some letters and answered some people by phone. 'Do people understand', he says, 'that they mustn't take up too much of your time?' 'Oh sure,' I say, 'they're great – with some exceptions.' I hope he'll take the hint, he doesn't: he obviously considers he's an exception to the exceptions. So he goes on and on, telling me about himself, and about his relationships with other people, and about his opinions, and about how stupid the world is . . . At length, I say, oh, what time is it? hoping again he'll get the message. Not our Denis. He says he hasn't the faintest idea what the time is, he doesn't wear a watch, he lives by the sun, he's so absolutely perfect, so totally in harmony with the universe . . . And he goes on talking about himself for half-an-hour. At the end of it all, with me squirming my toes in agony, and ready to throttle the bugger with his own phone cord, he says: 'I hope I've raised your spirits a little. You sounded a bit down in the dumps when you started talking: your voice sounded a bit tired.'

It's Boris again, this time from his new home 'between Korea and the China Sea'. It would be a little paradise there, he says, if it weren't for the bloody pirates – and the local population. He was coming in one night on his rubber dinghy from a bout of fishing when he saw this house, his own house, dammit, blazing with light. It turned out the local priest was holding a conventicle there, and his Philippina wife hadn't dared say no, such a thing being an honour, but our Boris didn't see it that way. All he wanted was a quiet meal, a quiet drink, a good read at a book and then to bed with his wife. So he told them all to go to hell, and fuckin' fast. They're beginning to turn against him in the community, he says. Maybe he'll go to Australia, somewhere around Darwin.

This time, it's Jacques Martinelli, a Franco-Italian, who lives in Brest. His grandfather, he told me months ago in a letter, was a friend of

Mussolini's in Italy, when they were both about nineteen years old.
But Jacques' grandfather was on the democratic republican Left,
whereas Mussolini was on the fascist Left. One day, Mussolini said
to Jacques' granda, when they were both drunk together: 'We'll have
to do something to get things right in this country. The people are
walking on their heads!' He was holding the newspaper upside
down . . . When Mussolini came to power, he told Jacques' grandfather he should scram, otherwise he would have to put him in the
calaboose. Which is why Jacques' family came to France, and finally
to Brest. Jacques phones usually when he's a bit drunk (otherwise, he
says, he wouldn't dare). 'Before I met up with your books, I'd lost faith
in everything. And I'm not the only one. You clear up the atmosphere, open up new tracks, new life-spaces . . . I'm just a drunk, I
know, but I know what I'm talking about. At the moment I'm right in
the middle of a really oceanic binge, I'm not too steady on my feet.
It's hard to keep an even keel at the best of times. My dog died
yesterday of a cancer – he was eighteen years old. The vet said he was
going to suffer a lot, so my wife took him to the clinic for a jag. I'm
dead sick at the whole idea; life can really be lousy, I'm on the verge
of total collapse. But I know what I'm saying.'

Boris, back now from his Philippine island, is telling me that things
have really become impossible there: 'I'm going to have a try at the
north of Australia.' He has a pal in Manilla, an ex-Laos type like
himself. To make a little cash, this guy has the idea of exporting to
Paris a race of dog found only in Australia: between a Yorkshire and a
fox-terrier . . . And Boris concludes: 'Don't forget you can ask me for
anything. This isn't just drunken talk.' A few months later, he calls me
from St Malo. He says he's become a total solitary – 'like everybody
else, only they don't know it'. His wife has gone back to the
Philippines, but he can't: he's become public enemy no. 1 there.
He'll get his things out of the Philippines by plane, leave the stuff
with a jazz singer he knows in Hong Kong, while he looks for a place

in Macao. So that's a plan. But he's also thinking seriously of doing himself in: 'Why keep on fuckin' around the stupid world, phoning up friends?' He then goes on: 'In the face of eternity, we're nothing at all.' That's right, Boris, I say, that's dead right. 'I won't bother you any more,' he says. But I know he will. The bugger knows I like him.

EVENING'S LITTLE IMAGES

All I ask from television is an unpretentious but not totally corny little film that will allow me to disconnect my mind from its labours between, say, half past eight and ten o'clock. At that time, I'll have been working ten, eleven, twelve hours: I'm too tired to do good work, but my brain's still active, the neurones are still doing the Highland fling. So all I want is a little series of images that will occupy it and let it cool down – so I can go quietly to sleep.

One might think this is a very modest request, and that I am bound to be satisfied.

Not so.

Television is turning into the cruddiest circus imaginable. Up till recently, you *could* find a decent little film somewhere, but no more. What you have now is various concoctions of 'Games, Music, Gaiety' and debate-shows that leave you with the disagreeable sensation that humanity delights in tedious baloney.

There are still films shown, I admit. But what films! Always the same stuff. Here's a typical menu. On TF1: *Panic in Town*, a 'classical thriller', starring Jean-Paul Belmondo; on A2, *The Big Job*, a 'conventional thriller' starring Jean-Paul Belmondo; on France 3, *Crime and Punches*, a 'nutty thriller', starring . . . Jean-Paul Belmondo. I don't want to suggest that Mister Belmondo has a monopoly of this astronomical crap: I'm just suggesting a certain monotony. If it isn't Jean-Paul doing his stuff, it's some other joker of the same calibre – or worse, much worse. I won't even mention the names of those who star in *The Numbskulls*, which was followed up recently by an equally great success, *The Nitwits*.

And new films are being made. Not only are they being made, they are being boosted. Their actors and actresses are regularly invited on the eight o'clock news, originally intended, I naively imagine, to tell us about significant events in the world. Not only are they asked to talk at length about their films, which, of course, as the commentator will say, are 'to be viewed and reviewed', they are asked their opinions about world affairs. The result, to say the least, is painful . . .

Even when a new channel starts up with better intentions, which happens now and then, pretty soon it's toeing the line, sliding down into the rut.

There are still, though, fortunately, exceptions.

Last week, for example, somebody had managed – no doubt while the boss wasn't looking – to programme Julien Duvivier's film *Le Paquebot Tenacity*, based on the play by Charles Vildrac, that goes back to 1933. I first saw that film years ago, at a hole-in-the-wall cinema in Paris. The copy I saw had been prepared for distribution in Japan, so that there were Japanese subtitles or rather side-titles, flickering at the right side of the screen all the time. As for the soundtrack, it sounded at times as if it had eggs frying on it, at others as if a hurricane was raging through it. And the images were all smudgy grey. But I loved it.

Le Paquebot Tenacity is the story (but what counts mainly of course is the *atmosphere*) of two out-of-work printers in Paris who have dreams of going away to far places and who have got hold of a prospectus put out by The Upper Canada Company offering trans-Atlantic passage and the wherewithal to settle in the wilds of Manitoba. One of the two mates, Bastien, is a gallus, enterprising type; the other, Alfred, is shy, hesitant, still not decided that he really wants to leave. 'What's keeping you back?!' cries Bastien. And Alfred, in his slow, quiet, dragging voice: 'Oh, nothing really, and, then, a bit of everything.' Alfred will say later that he loves places, and likes to take time to settle in to situations: if he went for a walk round the world, he says, he'd probably stop at the first stage, and spend ten years there, maybe his whole life. The film, in other words, is about the dialectics of staying–leaving, sedentariness–nomadism.

The mates leave for Le Havre: big harbour, rain falling on the quays, a little bordello, Louisette's Bar, and a hotel-restaurant, Cordier's, with its kind lady-owner and its pretty little skivvie, Thérèse. Our two companions meet old Hidoux, a gruff, burly bloke who makes a living doing odd jobs around the station and the harbour, and whose talk is all of destiny: 'Everybody lives like a cork on a stream.' Old Hidoux's dream has always been to have a clean, quiet room with a potted plant and a book, but what he has – that's *his* destiny – is a lousy dookit and a bottle of bad wine. It turns out he also is from Paris, from the Rue St-Maur. 'Ah, the Rue St-Maur', says Alfred nostalgically, 'that's where I used to spend my summer holidays, with my aunt.' Old Hidoux takes them to see the *Tenacity*, on which they're to make the trip – not as grand a boat as they had expected, but still impressive. Bastien tries to buck up his friend, talking enthusiastically about the life ahead of them, while Alfred still has 'more than one little regret'. The first departure is a fiasco: the boat has to turn back because of engine trouble. Repairs are going to take nobody knows exactly how long. The two mates get jobs at the harbour. And they both gravitate towards Thérèse: Alfred, sentimentally, Bastien, physically. With the result that it's finally Bastien who decides not to leave – he'll stick with Thérèse, become a street-hawker, while Alfred, unwilling to decide anything, preferring 'destiny' to do the deciding for him, finds himself alone on the ship as it leaves, feeling, wistfully, that he's been betrayed by his friend and Thérèse, but accepting his lot, and saying that for the first time since their dream started, he feels he really *wants* to leave. By way of consolation, old Hidoux tells him that maybe after all he's got the better part and the better way lying before him . . .

I've told the story, but I haven't described the atmosphere, which comes from the tones of the voices, the rain on the quays, ships' funnels hooting, and the music, now a discreet violin, now jazz trumpet, but especially the song that runs through the film, and which is all present there at the end as the SS *Tenacity* sails away into the sunrise:

> *Les chagrins traînent sur les quais*
> *C'est défendu d'les embarquer*
> *Nos chagrins, les gars, espérons*
> *Qu'ils seront morts quand nous r'viendrons.*

'We leave our sorrows lying on the quays, because it's forbidden to take them aboard; let's just hope, lads, that when we come back, our sorrows will be dead.'

Ah, if I could get a little film like that every evening!

But most of the time, there's nothing, absolutely nothing remotely resembling such a thing.

Now and again, there's a Western.

That suits me well enough.

Why?

Well, this isn't the place to give yet another history of the Western, say from Fenimore Cooper to Gary Cooper, in ten tall chapters, but maybe I can offer a little fragmentary phenomenology.

The first thing about the Western is space. After the long introductory statement ('These were the years immediately following the disaster of the Civil War'), you see a lone figure riding along the horizon. Going from nowhere to nowhere. But he's going to stop over somewhere for a while, just passing through. It's what happens when he stops that constitutes the incidents of the film, but it's essential to bear in mind the wider perspective: the man just passing through. A buddhist phrase has this: 'Alone you're born, alone you live, alone you die, and alone you hack out your path to nirvana.' The Western hero is that, in a kind of a way. When you see him close, he has the look of a contemplative, a vastness (that can narrow suddenly into sharp concentration) in his eyes, and there's an easy looseness (that can contract into lightning-fast activity) in his body. For the most contemplative is also, if need be, the most active. As Blaise Cendrars writes somewhere: 'Being a poet, I could get to reality faster than the other guy'.

Our man (call him Shane or Hondo, or just Hombre) enters the town, makes contact with civilisation . . . But there's no need to recount the whole story of any one film. That's not what matters. It's the repertoire of events, scenes, and gestures that counts, and the general space-thing – it's these that remain in the mind. In every film you recognise the same elements. One film may kaleidoscope them differently from another, there may be more or less finesse displayed in their use, but the elements are identical, and it is these that give the pleasure, with no extraneous thought-processes concerning plot, meaning, etc. There's nothing complicated about a Western. It is elementary. Elementary, but not stupid, not vulgar (just avoid, if possible, the sentimentality, buffoonery and bulldozer patriotism of a John Ford, for example), and most often not gratuitously violent, with blood and guts spurting all over the place. Not pretentious either, like so many films that would like to be more, and, not making it, just get on your nerves.

So, there's what I'm looking for, from my little image box in the evening, and I'm finding it less and less . . .

A friend tells me I should be technical about all this and increase my scope, give myself more chances, with more programmes. Another friend says: 'Why bother about television? If you want to disconnect, why not just get drunk, the way writers have done from time immemorial?'

Both my friends have points there.

I suppose that, by getting a bunch of parabolas fixed up on the house, and with two or three decoders to hand, I could tune into countless satellites and have a bigger pool of possibilities at my disposal – but would I bother to go fishing?

Ach, maybe I'll just buy a case of Scotch whisky and drown in tradition.

The Icelanders

I'm sitting in the bar *Le Pierre Loti*, watching the rain fall over Paimpol, watching it fall over the grey stone, over the grey-green waters of the harbour

I got into town late last night, and took a room at the *Hôtel des Chalutiers*.

This morning, early, I walked along the quay, past the old Iceland boat, the *Mad Atao*, past cafés and bars: the *Pierre Loti*, the *Neptune*, the *Islandais*, till I arrived at the Free French monument to seamen who met their death in the Second World War. There's a phrase of

General de Gaulle's engraved on the stone, beginning: 'Waves do not wear away granite.' Noble rhetoric, but bad geology (waves do most definitely erode granite), and therefore bad poetry, which is a pity, but the world is so full of stuff like that you take it for granted.

Continuing my morning walk, I came up against the window of a shop bearing, both in French and in German, a huge sign:

PHOTOGRAPHIES DU TEMPS D'ISLANDE
PHOTOS AUS DEN ISLÄNDISCHEN ZEITEN

As I came closer to the window, I saw that the brothers Torty had been taking and exhibiting photographs of Paimpol and the fishing boats that went up to Iceland, since 1898: 'Very careful work, not done in a hurry.' I had a good long look at the brown sepia photographs of the boats that used to go from here to Iceland for the cod fishing, and of the faces of the men that sailed and worked in them: faces marked with naïve wonder or with a cold, hard fatalism. I would have willingly talked a little with the present descendant of the Torty photographer-family, and went round to the side door, since the main door was closed. But the side door, despite my determined knocking, did not open. On it, however, was stuck a forbidding message, in the shape of a bit of faded paper on which was written in large, bold letters: 'The Lirzics better not show their faces here.'

For lunch, I hesitated between couscous at the *Bab-el-Oued* and cod at *Le Reykjavik*, and finally chose salmon at *La Paimpolaise*.

Now I'm sitting in the *Pierre Loti Bar*, in front of me a black, pungent coffee, looking out at the rain . . .

I'm seeing a house that trembles and shudders in the rain before taking on definition. It's in the straight-lined, white-walled, rain- and-sun drenched town of Rochefort, farther south down the Atlantic coast, in the Saintonge. At the window stands a young boy, listening to the strident cries of gulls in the immediate vicinity, in the distance the plaintive calls of marsh birds, and maybe the snatch of a sea-song down by the dockyards. He'll stand there listening, watching shadows dancing on a wall, then turn back to his table where he'll look through his collection of shells and pore over books on navigation, including the notebooks of his elder brother and his grandfather, full of details about Tonkin, the Barbary Coast, the Malay Straits . . .

The name of this young boy is Julien Viaud, later to be known as the writer Pierre Loti.

Why resuscitate Pierre Loti, that narcissistic little twerp, that naval pimp who, from the age of thirty on, used make-up to camouflage certain features of his physiognomy, that cultural cameleon who liked to dress up as a Turk, an Albanian, a Japanese, that superficial, supercilious dandy who delighted in displaying his loukoum loves, that snob who enjoyed hob-knobbing with addle-pated, scatter-brained aristocrats in the fin-de-siècle villas of Biarritz?

Well, let's look a little closer.

If you pass through the unprepossessing door of the house in Rochefort, you find yourself in a kind of architectural cosmorama: you move from a Renaissance room and a Gothic room to a Turkish room, a Bedouin room, a Muslim temple, an Egyptian library – at one time there was also a Chinese room and a Japanese pagoda. It's a profusion of object, colour and form, going from massive solidity through crimson splendour to slender arabesque . . . But at the top of the house, you come to Loti's private room: small, with bare white-washed walls, decorated only with fencing equipment and a piece of Arab calligraphy.

I'm interested in that sequence of spaces, and in that ultimate space, in a man's struggle with himself from confusion to clarity, and in a kind of writing.

Loti is one of those ghost-companions I've been reading and rereading here in the house of tides. He is a pilgrim on the face of the earth and in the fields of culture. It's the kind of pilgrimage that began with the peregrinations of the Romantic Self (Byron's *Childe Harold*, and so on) that goes through several phases: heroic, narcissistic, nihilistic, before it opens out, here and there, into a new nomadism.

Loti is, first and foremost, a narcissist. Before dismissing his narcissism out of hand, I'd suggest that, again, we take a closer look. I'd say Loti's narcissism is a kind of shadow-boxing, an activity that tunes up the muscles, improves one's locomotive style. At the same time, this 'shadow-boxing' is a self-assertion over against, not only social congestion, but, more deeply, over against total absorption in the infinite, or total collapse in the face of nothingness.

We can go then from shadow-boxing to shadow-writing: a writing that is a writing on the wall – testimonials from the abyss, apocalyptic opera, exultant and provocative revelation.

As a writer, Loti is the anti-Zola. To say such a thing is, for many, to marginalise him completely, with two pages in the chapter 'The late nineteenth-century novel: exotics and eccentrics' of some humdrum history of literature. I'd say on the contrary that it's in this he contributes to the opening of a new context. That most literature should still be sub-Zola is just one more sign that literature, on the whole, has not been moving as much as it might, has turned, in fact, into a very doughy, very dumpy mass. To put this in another way, if I find it hard to read *Madame Chrysanthème*, I can't read Zola at all; it wouldn't even occur to me to take him down from the shelves – he's up there with Dickens, who doesn't even descend any more at Christmas.

In reaction to the 'romantic novel', which, in the hands of the jobbers, had degenerated into a mere love story, Zola put forward the 'experimental novel', based on a stout plot, set in a conscientiously documented social setting (this year, the slaughterhouse, next year a hospital, a school, a railway depot . . .), the narrator functioning in flawless objectivity. That such productions can, at their best, be a contribution to sociology, there is no doubt. But they hardly satisfy all the faculties of a human being, hardly employ all the mobility of the human mind. They always go on at one level, for one thing, and with the same tone.

Contrast to this the Loti method, or rather, as I would like to call it, the cosmopoetic method, of which Loti's work is a minor, but interesting, manifestation.

In the first place, intrigue, imbroglio, considered as mere nuisance, is thrown to the winds. What takes over is itinerary, for example 'a long walk in the infinity of the desert'. Then, all kinds of heterogeneous materials come in. At one point, in the progression of *Rarahu* (published as *Le Mariage de Loti*, the editor being afraid that the original title, hard to pronounce, hard to remember, would scare off the public), in which, among other matters, Loti tells the story of a transient marriage on Tahiti, he sticks in great chunks of a French–Maori dictionary. Elsewhere, it will be a wad of ethnological, botanical, pharmaceutical information: what Loti called 'pedantic digressions' (from every trip he made, he would come back with a 'voluminous notebook' – there definitely a man after my own heart!), the whole written with various tones, and using several types of language, at times several languages, in a polyphonic play of energy. Although his editor stuck the label on them, Loti isn't writing novels at all, nor mere 'travel books'. He himself preferred the term *récits sauvages* ('wild narratives'), and a friend of his said that there'd be no name for what he was doing until literary criticism was taken over by chemists, paleontologists and veterinarians specialising in whales.

If Loti, writing all the time, passed through Tahiti (*Rarahu*), Turkey (*Aziyadé*), Montenegro (*Pasquala Ivanovitch*), China (*The Last Days of Peking*), and Japan (*Japoneries d'automne*), the Basque country (*Ramuntcho*), it's perhaps with Brittany that his name is most associated – in fact, as he says himself, a lot of Parisians took him for a Breton. That's because of the trilogy: *Mon frère Yves* ('My brother

Yves'), *Matelot* ('At sea') and, especially, *Pêcheur d'Islande* ('The Iceland fisherman').

Loti first got to know Brittany when he was a naval cadet in Brest, between 1867 and 1869. He was impressed by the landscape: the salty greyness, the lichened rocks, the windbent trees – and the town of Paimpol. In 1877 he met Pierre Le Cor, who was quartermaster on the *Tonnerre*, based then in Lorient, and that friendship (Pierre Le Cor was to become 'my brother Yves') strengthened his ties with Brittany. Then, in 1882, he met a young girl, who'd come to see her brother aboard the *Surveillance* stationed in Brest, and fell hopelessly in love with her: 'A fisher girl, tanned by the sea, of that type known in the Côtes-du-Nord as the Icelanders.' He went to see her at her home, out for nothing more at first than a little fling, but he was turned away, with a look of scorn, because this girl didn't want to be just another officer's plaything. He came back at her again, this time offering marriage, but was spurned once more. That was the time, near Christmas, when, back from her house, he wandered distraught through the streets of Paimpol, and even went into a church, maybe feeling that he could get in touch with the girl via her faith. Years later, he saw her again, on a road near Paimpol, married by now, but she nevertheless allowed him to kiss her on the cheek. All this time, the idea of a book was growing in Loti's mind, a book about the Iceland fishing of Paimpol. Then, in 1883, he met Pierre Le Scoarec on board the *Atalante*, who was to become the model for Yann Gaos, the main protagonist of *Pêcheur d'Islande* . . .

It was the codfishing in the waters of Iceland that marked more than anything else the old life of Paimpol. Every year, a hundred boats and more, out from 'the head of the pool' (what Paimpol, *Penpoull*, means in Breton), would be moving for five months through the Iceland mists. The system of payment being piecework, the men would tear out the tongues of the cod they fished and put them in a wicker basket, from which, at the end of the day, they'd be counted by the skipper. You have to imagine men sliding about for twenty hours at a stretch in a bloody slush, each man at a hole through which his line passed, a hole for which he'd picked a number out of a hat, or had gambled for with dice, since some were more favourable than others, and at a few you could even rig up a little shelter against the rain and the wind. The hooks, seven inches long, on which you attached your bait, were often rusty, so that your hands would be sore with whitlows and boils. As to your eyes, they were seared with wind and wet and salt, so that, in addition to all the rest, you risked going blind, and often did.

'There were five of them, sturdy fellows, with their elbows on the table, drinking, in a dark little hole that smelt of brine.' That's how Loti's *Pêcheur d'Islande* begins, and what follows is a kind of folk ballad in prose, and a hymn to sea, darkness and death. 'The foc'sle narrowed at one end, like the inside of a gutted gull, and it swayed slightly, giving a faint creak . . .'

I was reading the book in the room of my Paimpol hotel. Outside, a high north wind was blowing.

The next morning, I continued my trip beyond Paimpol, to the eastern tip of the north coast.

Over by the Arcouest headland stands a chapel. In its porch are hung marble tablets bearing the *in memoriam* of 'Icelanders' lost at sea. It's a litany of annihilation: 'To the memory of Sylvestre Bernard, captain of *The Mathilda*, lost at the age of 33 in Iceland during the storm that blew from 5 to 8 April 1867, along with the 18 men of his crew'; 'In memory of Silvestre Camus, who fell overboard and disappeared, in the region of the Norden Fiord, in Iceland, aged 18'; 'To the memory of Jean Louis Floury, aged 27, a seaman aboard *The Marguerite*, lost in Iceland 8th August 1879' . . .

It's at Arcouest that you take the boat for the Isle of Bréhat, *Enez Vriad*.

Bréhat is a tousled little island, with a chaos of red and rosy rocks, potato fields surrounded by bluebells, the song of a cuckoo in the woods, and gull cries that echo through space, time and human consciousness.

It's said that it was here Columbus met a seaman who told him how to get to the New World.

An Old Owl's Nest

Ⅰf ever there was a provincial hole, a cavern of obscurity, a cess-pool of piety, a bog of despondency, a morass of morosity, a cultural cul-de-sac and an old owl's nest, it is Tréguier, the ancient and venerable capital of the Trégor.

And yet, and yet . . .

It was here, in the fifth century, that a travelling Welsh monk by the name of Tudwal founded a place of light upon a hill. It was here, in the thirteenth century, that St Yves was born, man of law, patron saint of widows, orphans and the poor. In the fifteenth century, Tréguier was the first burg in the West to have a printing press: in

1485, they printed a compendium of Breton law, *La coutume de Bretagne*, and in 1499, the *Catholicon*, a dictionary bringing together Latin, French and Breton. Then, to crown it all, here in Tréguier, in 1823, was born one of the intellectual lights of the nineteenth century, Ernest Renan.

The statue of Ernest Renan stands, provocatively (for in the stuffy nineteenth century his name smelled of free-thinking sulphur), right in front of the cathedral: a paunchy dwarf of a figure, with a big head, leaning slightly to the left, holding a stick. Looming behind him, bearing aloft a laurel wreath, a tall slender idealistic figure, no doubt that of the goddess Athena . . .

What happens with any great thinker and writer such as Renan is that they get mummified: a public image forms of them which they themselves often encourage (it is difficult to remain an individual, outside all the coteries, cliques and clans), becoming, in the process, caricatures of themselves. Then, they get pigeonholed, sometimes by their disciples and followers, who tend to 'translate' them on a lower key, but mostly by the composers of superficially conceived and often hastily written histories of literature and of ideas, which, at best, offer only a preliminary approach. This goes on until another habitual phenomenon occurs: someone comes along who is out to debunk the whole thing. Meanwhile, of course, the work, which alone counts through time, lies in obscurity, its energies unemployed, its working lines dormant.

The debunker of Ernest Renan, the man who set out to knock him right off his pedestal, was Maurice Barrès, in his *Eight Days with Mr Renan*, originally an 'essay in picturesque criticism' published in the *Revue de Paris et de Saint-Petersbourg*.

That Barrès admires Renan, there is no doubt: you don't take the trouble to write 'picturesque criticism' about someone you despise — you either don't talk about him at all, or you make a slight reference in passing. For Barrès, Renan is one of the 'tough animals', perhaps more elephantine than lionesque, endowed with 'the clearest and most well-equipped intelligence I've ever known' and able to be charming when he cares, but also hiding behind a smiling and benevolent exterior a resignation to the fact that most human life is irredeemably trivial. Barrès also obviously respects Renan's conception of literature: that hardly anyone writes anything really significant before the age of forty, that a country can be stifled by hordes of little literati and by armies of journalists, and that what counts is not just novels and a few lyrics, but the extension of historical and naturalist studies up into the area of a transcendentally poetic work.

Where the irony comes across is, first of all, in the physical description of the 'illustrious author': he has a grotesque head, a bishop's belly and a ponderous, arthritic walk. This would be superficial, even obnoxiously irrelevant, were it not for the fact that this bulky little monster is frequently surrounded by half-naked young ladies who invite him cooingly to tell them all about Love and Passion, an invitation with which the Master complacently complies, providing the damsels with a syrupy pabulum that has them delightfully titillated and deliciously enthralled. It's this hypocritical priesterliness, this ecclesiastical unction that Barrès shows up, as well as Renan's heavy Breton localism: his sentimental recalling of how his mother would call him 'Ernestic'; his enthusing about 'the simple soul of the people'; and his desire to be received into 'the Breton tradition'. Barrès even suggests in a humorous sketch that, in purgatory where he dwells, Renan is worried silly that the setting up of his statue in front of the cathedral will prevent that ultimate pantheonic merger.

Leaving Renan to his personal fate (but I know I'll be getting into his real work later), I enter the cathedral. The main feature there, a place of worship and the focal point for pilgrims, is the tomb of St Yves: a monument of white marble in a glass chamber, with candles flickering and guttering all around, and, along with three model boats, a multitude of votive tablets, *'Thanks to Saint Yves'*, *'Good Saint Yves, who gave me my son and kept him safe for me, watch over him please always.'*

Outside again, coming down the steps past three tramps with bloated, winey faces asking for alms, while choughs wheel round the cathedral spire, alighting on chimneys and TV aerials, I see, along the pavement behind the statue of Renan, three butchers' shops, three pastry-shops, a *Maison de la Presse*, a bar called *Le Pénalty*, and a bookshop which used to sell only books, but which now sells books and crockery, mostly heavy, thick-lined colourful plates from Quimper.

In the Librairie Tanguy, ethereally full of harp music, I find books such as *L'Âme bretonne* ('The Breton soul') by Le Goffic, *La légende de la mort chez les Bretons armoricains* ('The death legend among the Bretons of Armorica') by Anatole Le Braz and the six thick volumes of *Histoire de la Bretagne* ('A history of Brittany') by A. de la Borderie and B. Pocquet. I do not find what I am vaguely looking for: the books of Comte Hyacinthe du Pontavier de Heyssey, who was born at Tréguier in 1814 and died at London in 1876, translator of Byron, author of *Nuits rêveuses* ('Dream-filled nights'), *Études et aspirations* ('Studies and aspirations'), *Sillons et débris* ('Flotsam and jetsam') . . .

Walking through the streets and backstreets, the lanes and vennels of the town. Past the many fine mansions with their great doors: the convent of the *Communauté des Sœurs du Christ* ('the Sisters of Christ'), now an old folks' home; the Renan house, now a museum; and the smaller houses with frilly, furtive, white-lace curtains in their windows. Till, away down a back-lane in the half-dark, I end up dialoguing silently with an anonymous, history-less cat, whose eyes, full of galactic emptiness, reflect the light of the moon now rising behind the roofs.

On the Ramparts

of St Malo

I t was another of those old travelling monks that founded St Malo. His name was Maclou, and he built himself a den on the sea-girt rock called Aaron . . .

It's of him I think mainly this January afternoon as I walk round the ramparts of St Malo.

He certainly didn't come alone.

In fact, you have to imagine whole flotillas coming round by the Celtic Sea and across the Channel, with some big sail-boats at the centre, and, scattered all around them, little craft made of wicker and hide.

After the sailing, the settling.

When Cado was ready to set up his monastery at Nant-Carban, he came across a boar that ran off at the sight of him, but stopped three times before disappearing. Cado stuck branches in the ground at the three spots. On the first spot, he built his church; on the second, the refectory; and round the third were built the individual cells.

When Lunar or Leonarius arrived in Armorica in 535, a few miles from the mouth of the Rance, the land was covered with forest. Lunar liked the forest, but he had a problem: how to feed his folk. Monks weren't supposed to hunt, nor could they fish. Then, one day, Lunar saw a bird, and that bird had an ear of corn in its mouth. *'Great!'* thought Lunar, or rather: *'Benedicite omnia opera Domini, laudate et superexaltate eum in saecula!'* He then asked the bird, in the name of the Lord Jesus-Christ, to lead him to the corn. Which the wee bird obligingly did.

To come back to Malo, when he arrived in Dumnonia (north Brittany – but you find the same word on the west coast of Scotland), around 550, his first action was to stage a midnight mass, which all the pagans of the district, with their chief Conomor at their head, came to look at and listen to, amazed.

That's how the town of St Malo got on to the map.

I used to frequent a second-hand bookshop in St Malo, called *Septentrion*, in which I'd flip through old books concerning the town and its inhabitants and the many maritime expeditions that took place from it. It was out of the way stuff I was after, not the standard histories, not the spate of historical novels the town has given rise to.

In one of those old books, I came across a long poem, written in pithy, fifteenth-century English, called 'The Libel of English Policies' (*Libellus de politia conservativa maris*), the aim of which was to 'exhort all England to keepe the sea and namely the narrowe sea' against her strongest enemies, those 'rovers on the sea' of 'pety Britaine', concentrated like crows in the said city of Malo:

Furthermore to write I am faine
Somewhat speaking of the little Britayne.

. . .

And of this Britaine, who so trueth lovis,
Are the greatest rovers and the greatest theevis

. . .

Thys they have bene in divers coasts many
Of our England, more then rehearse can I:
In Norfolke coastes, and other places about,
And robbed and brent and slaine by many a rowte

. . .

For Britayne is of easie reputation;
And Saincte Malo turneth hem to reprobation . . .

So, first, there were monks.

Then, seamen and explorers and pirates.

Thereafter, the poet Chateaubriand, with all this in him.

Chateaubriand liked to stand up here on the ramparts as a young boy and 'gaze into the blue distances'.

And in his life he was going to try and reconcile two contradictory tendences: 'Wanderer on the face of the world as I may be, I have the sedentary tastes of a monk.'

He's not the only one.

When, in August 1944, General Patton, with the 8th Army Corps, was making for Brest after the landing in Calvados and the Avranches breakthrough, he was afraid of a flank attack coming from St Malo. Believing that the fortress was crammed with German troops, he got together a task-force whose mission was to blast St Malo to smithereens. Which, after three weeks, was accomplished. As the result of a hail of incendiary bombs, the town was left a heap of smoking ashes, while Patton kept marching on.

Within the next few years, St Malo was built up again, as near as possible to old plans. 'It has lost its archives, but not its soul,' wrote the local culture-representative.

Along with its sister-rocks, the Grand Bey and Île de Cézembre, the Ouvras, the Roches aux Anglais, the Pierres aux Normands, the Rats and the Queue des Rats, the Herbiers, the Pierres de la Saratte, the Letruns, the Patouillets and the Carolines, St Malo's rock stands witness to a whole coastline that has disappeared. The impact of the waves, the force of the tide, the pressure of the currents have been such that only a few blocks of rough granite have managed to resist them. Nowhere in the world (except for the estuary of the Severn in England and the Bay of Fundy in Nova Scotia) is the distance between the high tide mark and the low tide mark so great, the result being that every six hours the landscape changes completely. At low tide, wide stretches of sand are laid bare. Up till recently you could come across on them the remains of the ancient coastal forest. The old inhabitants of St Malo would go out looking for bits of a very hard black wood that they used for the construction of their espaliers.

It is, I realise, a very fragmentary kind of meditation that's been going through my head as I've been walking round the ramparts of St Malo, from the Porte Saint-Vincent to the Tour Bidouane, and from there to the Champs Vauverts and the Porte de Dinan.
   If I'm to get it all rounded out, maybe I better go round again.

ALONG THE MARGINS

My idea, vague enough at the beginning, was to go on a walking tour between the Baie de Sainte-Marguerite and the town of Morlaix, along the *abers*.

An *aber* is a valley invaded by the sea. There are three of them up behind Brest: the Aber-Ildut, the Aber-Benoît and the Aber-Wrac'h.

Thinking of them now, I have an image of white sand sifted by the wind, of long lines of black seaweed, piles of rough red rock, clumps of blue thistles, hordes of crying gulls, and solitary, silent cormorants . . .

Here's the notebook of that late summer trip.

I pass the long dunes of Sainte-Marguerite and come along the Baie des Anges with its dancing lights. In the little harbour of the Aber-Wrac'h, I hang about the quay for a while, before going to look for a pancake-house. There's an old black and white three-master moored a few yards off shore and I ask a man who, like myself, is standing beside the shelter belonging to the *Hospitaliers Sauveteurs Bretons* what such a boat is still doing in these parts.

'It's Father Jaouen' he says.

'That the name of the ship?'

'No, it's the name of the skipper. He takes drug-addicts from the big cities out to sea.'

Thus informed, I go and eat my daily *crêpe*, then cross the bridge over the Aber, making for Plougerneau, where I intend to spend the night.

Up at dawn, ('dawn', in Breton, is *gwazhenn-an-deiz* – I've got Roparz Hémon's little Breton–French dictionary in my rucksack), I leave for the Grèves de Lilia.

Place-names in general intrigue me, and I'm especially intrigued here. Yesterday, Aber-Wrac'h was pure Breton, pure Celtic (the *wrac'h* syllable, meaning 'witch', is what you find up in Scotland in the name of a tide-race off the coast of Mull: *Corrievreckan*). But 'Lilia'? – it sounds Italian. And, consulting the map, further on I see 'Grèves de Zorn', which looks a lot like German.

The little village of Lanvaon is still wrapped in summer mist. And the same with Tréguestan. But when I get to the port of Lilia, the mist has evaporated and it's clear shining light all along the coast and out to sea. The Île Vierge lighthouse stands sturdily on its rocky islet, flanked by two conscientious little aolian wind-engines, and a fisherman is rowing his punt towards the smack called *Pax et labor*.

When I get back on to the road again, it's to make off in the direction of the Grève St-Michel.

All this Breton 'far west' used to be called, and by some still is, the 'coast of legend'.

It's true enough that, in the old days, there were stories and legends here galore. And the imagination involved in them was often of a macabre nature. You would hear, for example, about severed hands scuttling across the moor with their thumbs in the air – like a crab out hitchhiking.

I won't deny the interest of these tales. To every age its cinema. But now and then you do feel the need to do a little scrape-job on all this 'culture'. For often enough a plain and simple tale has been over-loaded with a fantastic superstructure. Especially when Christianity has been at it. A friend who now lives in Nantes, but who comes from these shores, told me a story about a young girl who, every evening, went down to the beach to have carnal intercourse with the 'red prince', that is, of course, the devil. 'Bullshit, church-crap', said Mona the Nantaise. The 'red prince' is obviously enough a metaphor for the sunset, and what more natural for a fisherman's daughter to want to have a good look at the setting sun, so as to have some notion of the next day's weather? And if she felt like having a little naked dance to herself down there on the beach while she was at it, once again, what more natural?

Let's have less swollen imagination, and a little more pelagian inspiration!

I don't think of these shores as the 'legend coast', but as the 'seaweed coast'. There really is a lot of wrack here, and it's always been part of the local economy: 'wrack-gatherer', they tell me, is even a trade that's coming back. In the old days, they burnt it for potassium, and from May to June you'd see heavy smoke drifting from seaweed furnaces all the way from Quiberon to Saint-Brieuc Bay. But exploitation is one thing, knowledge is another. I'm thinking of Jens Peter Jacobsen, the author of the world-weary novel *Niels Lyhne*, but also of a pathfinder thesis: *A critical and systematic survey of the seaweeds of Denmark*. I've started studying the seaweeds of Brittany myself, from the *sargassum* recently arrived in these waters to *palmaria palmata*, and from there to *laminaria*. Seaweeds are more interesting than novels! Mosses are more enlightening than legends! And when you think of all the crap poured into children's ears over the centuries (about 'big bad wolves' and all the rest), you wish the tale-telling would stop, and that kids got something better to think about.

At Kergoff, just for the sake of a little friendly talk, I drink a coffee before walking along Zorn strand and saluting the Black Island (*Enez Du*), as I make my way towards Le Curnic, Nodéven and Guissény, where I have a meal in the local pancake-house, *Ty ar Krampouz*.

When I get to Brignogan, about fifteen kilometres farther on, I gaze long upon the magnificent menhir surmounted by its ridiculous little cross, wonder if I'm going to check out the delights of the café called *Le Moonlight*, then decide to look right away for a nice quiet place to sleep on the Grève des Chardons Bleus.

The wind is lifting the white sand. Just above the tide-line, I find several of those crabs called 'tight-rope walkers' (*coryestes cassivelaunus*) and, in a pool among the rocks, several anemones (*actinia equina, actinia fragasea*).

They call the country up there the *'pays pagan'*, because it stayed outside the progress of Christian civilisation as long as it could, and was known as a country of savages and wreckers. The local folk would fix a lantern on the horns of a bull and let it wander along the wildest cliffs, so that ships out at sea would think it was a light indicating safety and refuge and bring their craft in against the rocks, where the populace would be waiting for it.

Of course, things have changed, but the northern 29ers (29, the number of this Finisterrian department) still have the reputation of a wild bunch. At Nodéven, I meet a red-haired lad with green eyes who wears a badge: M. I. B. I ask him what the letters mean: '*Mouvement des*

Insoumis Bretons' (the Breton movement of the unsubdued), he tells me defiantly.

I quit Brignogan early down the morning, passing through Plounéour-Trez, Goulven, Keremma, and along by Kernic Bay.

From Plouescat, with its splendid market-hall on Général-de-Gaulle square, the D 10 road strikes more or less straight for St-Pol-de-Léon – I can already see the slender spires of the town rising against the sky. But I make a detour by the coast, going from Plouescat to Poulfoën and from there to Kervalfou and Kérouzéré, before coming back to the main road and heading for Roscoff.

It's raining this morning on Roscoff, and the town is the colour of oysters. I'm tempted to take refuge in a café, or, maybe better still, in a hotel, but I board the little boat, the *Santez Anna*, that does a ferry run between Roscoff and Île de Batz (*Enez Vas*).

Mist, rain, black rocks, foam . . .

The crossing isn't long, about twenty minutes, but I've got the time to take a good look at a strangely attractive seascape: a hundred or so abrupt black rocks and round them, doing a wild jig, a very green sea, before setting foot on earth again and starting out along the path that goes round the island.

Little white-sand beaches, like scythe-blades, like crescent moons. Grey rocks covered with orange lichen. On the moor, gorse bushes hung with spiders' webs. And that little white plant that smells of honey, the samphire.

The sky has suddenly cleared, so that the wet sand has turned blue, and when I climb up to the top of the lighthouse, I can see Brignogan away there to the west and, towards the south-east, the chairs of Primel.

In the eastern corner of the island I come across the ruins of the Ste-Anne chapel, dug out of the sand in which they'd for long lain buried. On the walls of the chapel, two ex-votos: one, a painting showing a French boat being helped by a Spanisher and huge green waves threatening them both; the other, a simple tablet bearing these words: *'Reconnaissance à Ste-Anne, 1914–1918'*.

On my way back to the harbour to board the *Santez Anna*, I come across another tablet, fixed to the wall of one of the more modest houses of the island: 'The pilot Yves Tremintin, who distinguished himself with Bisson aboard the *Panayoti* on 4 Nov. 1827, died in this house on 3 June 1862. The population will not forget.'

I sleep at Roscoff in a hotel just along from the Mary Stuart house.

On the following morning, I find the five kilometres that separate Roscoff from St-Pol-de-Léon very long and very monotonous. Maybe that's why I leave the present and dig back into my memories

The first French people I ever knew came from this corner of Léon. The man we called 'the Onion Johnnie' would turn up once a year in our Scottish village, and he'd be expected. There he'd be knocking at the door, with his black beret, his brown stub of a cigarette and his bicycle bearing two big bunches of red-golden onions hanging from its handlebars.

'You want onion?' he would say.

My mother would always buy some, and send him on his way again with an *au revoir* or a *bon voyage* . . .

Here I am now on the Budès-de-Guébriant square in St-Pol, facing the dark cathedral where one can still see the little door for lepers and the solemn pulpit from which excommunications were delivered.

Outside St-Pol, I'm tempted by the Yokohama Bar, but walk on resolutely to the Pont de la Corde that crosses the estuary of the Penzé. The sky is slate blue. Then all at once a rainbow appears, followed soon by another.

At Carantec, I stand for a while contemplating the geological and atmospherical beauties of the Bay of Morlaix, then make for Le Frout – you see a lighthouse rising there right in the middle of the moor –

Kerozal, Ros-ar-Scour and Loquénolé and, finally, the good town of Morlaix (in Breton: Montroulez).

Morlaix lies huddled under its imposing viaduct

I pass a restaurant, *Au Passé Simple*, then a cakeshop with an extraordinary rococo front all white and gold, and the *Grand Café de La Terrasse*, which, I have been told, is the favourite meeting place of the literary and intellectual minds of the town.

In the museum, I admire the wooden-sculpted, white-painted effigy of a good-looking saint with big eyes (St Pol, of course), and linger awhile in front of some old sea-charts and some model boats. I also take the opportunity of saluting the poet Tristan Corbière, whose portrait (pipe, red cap, cutter and rough green sea) is hanging over there in a dark corner.

I then come back to the terrace of the *Grand Café*.

I first read the work of Tristan Corbière in Glasgow when, among other things, I was a student of French literature. At the time, I was reading also T. S. Eliot, the latter-day saint of the modern 'wastelands', who, right from the beginning of the century, had turned to Corbière in his attempt to remedy what he called a 'dissociation of sensibility' that had marked English poetry since the seventeenth century, with thought tending to go one way, towards artificial abstraction, and emotion to another, into sentimentality. Result: a singular type of schizophrenia that could only find some kind of relief in the numb platitudes of the novel or the chatterboxing of a certain social theatre: the thing was, beyond that split, to get back on to the ground of what might be called the *idea-sensation*.

That's what I tried to get at myself, via the translation of Corbière's poems, via the study of several grammars and philosophies, and via long hours of wandering either in the streets of my native city or along the west coast. That's how, step by step, bit by bit, the Firth of Clyde joined forces with the Baie des Trépassés and the fractured coastline of western Scotland linked up with the broken coasts of

Brittany. In that way too, not only was I able to navigate with more and more ease and pleasure between the two languages, but, on the basis of the two languages in question, I had the impression of approaching one more universal – the way the Dordogne and the Garonne join to form the Gironde and thereby mingle their waters with the Atlantic ocean . . .

I remember the first time I visited Armorica. I'd come from Nantes, on foot (with an occasional bout of hitch-hiking), and I was making for Roscoff:

> Old buccaneers' hole, old pirates' nest
> Where the wild Atlantic tempest roars
> Enjoy your well-deserved granite rest
> While the sea licks away at your cellar doors . . .

Already at Morlaix, I was on the lookout. It was there that Tristan's father (born in Brest, 1793) had settled in 1840 (he founded there the *Compagnie des paquebots du Finistère*, which linked Morlaix to Le Havre) and it was there Corbière was born five years later and where he was to die thirty years after. In a building that looked public and official (was it the townhall, or some assembly room? – I can't remember) I asked an initial question about the famous (at least for me) native son. I really got told where to get off. They were setting up a big exhibition on the 1914–18 war, no time to waste on the poet Corbière. I went away, thinking of one of Tristan's poems, *'La pastorale de Conlie'*, in which he evokes those Bretons called up to defend France against Prussia, but whom the government had thought fit to encamp in wretched conditions at Conlie, where so many men died in the mud and cold – a government scared that if it gave them anything else to exercise with but rusty old American Civil War rifles bought second hand from the US army, those Breton 'savages' might use them for some anti-national insurrection.

Leaving what he thought of as a lousy context behind him,

Corbière holed up here in Brittany in what he called his *Casino des Trépassés* ('the ghost casino'):

'It's an ancient tower, still standing, but headless. Its crown lies fallen at its feet. Crumbling ruins in drunken shapes are piled up all around, out of reach of the rising tide, protected from the snell and scouring gale [. . .], Oh! what a high, wild life we'll live there, my masters, guests of the house!'

At the end of the nineteenth century, a lot of poets were holing up in a similar way. It's Mallarmé's silent study; it's Nietzsche's mountain inn; it's Segalen's Chinese 'room of porcelain'. All in all, a kind of general poetic hibernation.

Probably too early yet to say it's Spring.

But who knows?

The tides of man . . .

Outside once more in the streets of old Morlaix after this little café meditation, I pass by the house of the Duchesse Anne, the *Macao Pub*, the *Bar Sympa-Ty* which houses the old seamen's club, a pancake-house called *Les Passagers du Vent* and the bookshop *Kornog*, which is sending out over the air the wild strains of an Irish fiddle.

So, there, in a handful of scattered shore-notes, is my *aber* trip.

With those Breton *abers* behind me, and that Irish music all around me, and a feeling for poetic mind-opening margins in my brain, I send out cosmical salutations to Aberystwyth and Aberdeen.

On the Paris–Brest

For years now, since, in addition to enjoying the hermit and beachcomber life, I also do a little poetico-cultural talking at the Sorbonne, I have been a great frequenter of the trains (first the Corail, all orange-grey-yellow, lately the aerodynamic silver-grey TGV of the Atlantic line) that run between Brest and Paris, and which I pick up at Plouaret.

To get to Plouaret, I travel from Lannion on the little green and white TER (*train express regional*).

Lannion station, on a Wednesday morning. The hour drawing

close, the driver gets into his cabin as one of the station hands goes along the platform to bring down the level-crossing barrier.

The train for Plouaret is about to leave. All aboard!

The little train pulls, shudders, throbs, and then gets into its putter-putter stride. The track is lined with rock surrounded by dark-green whin and russet-brown fern. Let's say it's early December, a blue, diamantine morning, puff cloud in the sky, the fields harrowed, above them crows, magpies, gulls. Now and then you get a glimpse of some greystone cottage nestled in a little valley. And at one point or another, for no apparent reason, the little TER will get all excited and rattle along at a greater rate than usual.

A grey granite spire, a cluster of dewy-white houses, and it's Plouaret.

I wait on the platform opposite the *Café de l'Abattoir*: the twittering of birds, an occasional phrase in Breton . . .

The other day, at Plouaret, a small man wearing a battered felt hat, with a bristly red moustache and teeth all brown and crooked, came up to me. He spoke with a hoarse voice and was obviously more than a bit drunk. He told me he'd been there on the platform at half past nine, well in time for the nine fifty. It wasn't that he had missed it, it was just that it hadn't turned up: 'They were on strike, the bastards.' So he went to phone 'the little lady', his wife, who lives at Quintin (he lives at Ploumanac'h, where he works on the life-saving boat – spends fifteen days at his place, fifteen days at hers). He phoned her up to say he'd be late – he was supposed to be at Quintin for the midday meal. She was in a bad tid about it, said he wasn't to turn up plastered, she knew he'd pass the time at some bar or other. Which, of course, he had, at the one just across the road. He'd gone over with his dog. That was his dog there, a little Scotch-terrier, attached by its leash to his case. 'He's a fine wee lad,' he says. 'Six years old.' He has to pay half price for him on the train. Sometimes he sits him up on a seat. One day a damned ticket-inspector – 'Ach, there are some decent ones, too' – objected and made a fuss. Anyway, when the compartment is full, he always puts the wee fella out in the corridor. He sits there, and doesn't budge an inch. 'If I got on the train first, he'd come right after me, dragging that case with him, even if it throttled him.' One day a woman with a kid sitting next to him asked if his dog was good-tempered. 'Good-tempered?' he said. 'Let me tell you, lady, he's already saved two kiddies from drowning, your wean has nothing at all to fear from him.' He's done, in fact, a lot of life-saving, at Ploum (Ploumanac'h), at Erquy, and elsewhere too. 'That wee dog', he says, 'has done St Malo and Lorient as well.'

The Rennes train was announced.

The express train from Brest bound for Rennes is about to enter the station. This train connects at Rennes with the TGV for Paris.

I'm in the Brest–Paris, Paris–Brest train about twenty-five times a year. In the last ten years, that makes a total of five hundred journeys . . .

From Plouaret to Rennes, at least at the hour I usually travel, it's a Corail train, that throbs less than the little TER, sways more.

For a while, it was always a saloon carriage. But recently, they seem to have brought back older rolling-stock, so that I'm in a compartment carriage. If I'm alone in it, fine. But if you're not alone in a compartment, you're more aware of the neighbours' talk than in the saloon. This morning, I'm all alone. I pull up the little tray-table from its blue-painted metal sheath, and get down to work. I usually do quite a lot of reading on the train.

Little grey houses or larger whitewashed houses, the first with lichen on their slate roofs, the latter still clean . . . This morning, we're hurtling through chill blue clarity, but I like it too when rain spatters over the window.

We have a couple of minutes stop at Guingamp: a thin steeple there to the left, and G. MAZEAS in big red letters on a building to the right.

Ladies and gentlemen, we are now arriving at Saint-Brieuc. This is a two-minute stopover. Saint-Brieuc, a two-minute stopover.

Two Breton businessmen have just got on the train, and they've come into my compartment. 'It's fine to have ideas', says one, 'but you've got to know how to implement them . . . To make roads is good for business . . . We've got to try and keep the grey matter in the country.'

I go to the bar for a coffee. A guy just before me has asked for a coca-cola. 'There you go,' says the barman, putting the can on the counter, 'Texas beaujolais!'

Back in my compartment, the businessmen are still talking, so I take out my notebook and write up the journey in it. If I can't concentrate on something else, I start noting everything. It's astonishing, the details you notice that way, and the sharp sense of reality you get. Most of the time, it's just a general fuzz.

Ladies and gentlemen, we are now coming to Rennes, the terminus of this train. Connection with the TGV for Paris. Please make sure you have left nothing in the compartment.

At Rennes, I go down from my arrival platform into the subterranean passage, and emerge again into the light of day at Platform 6, where the Atlantic TGV is waiting, all the long silver-grey carriages of it.

Ladies and gentlemen, good morning. You are now on board the Atlantic TGV bound for Paris-Montparnasse, with stops at Laval and Le Mans. Departure is imminent. Watch out for the automatic closure of the doors.

It looks as though it's going to be a quiet trip, this time. All my neighbours have their heads buried in newspapers.

I make some headway with my book . . .

That's when the American starts up, somewhere at the back of the saloon, and loudly, as if he was on the other side of the Rockies:

'I'm a rancher, a cowboy: Gary Cooper – *oui?* . . . What *départ'-mong?*' Somebody says '35, Ille-et-Vilaine'. 'Ah, *tray joli!* Where's the border? Normandy?' We then learn that he has cousins in Biarritz, where he usually visits, but this time he went to Roscoff. 'I love your country. *Tray joli!* Brittany! Tristan and Isolde, *oui?* I'm a Wagnerite! Exactly, *oui, oui* . . . Saint-Brieuk, that's an interesting name, *n'est-ce-pas?* How do you pronounce it?' Somebody answers, pronouncing very precisely: 'Saint-Brieuc'. *'Ah, oui. Exact'mong!'* I think that is maybe the end of it, but Gary Cooper is positively bubbling over with communicativeness. 'Those brown and white cattle, *quel type?'* Somebody says: *'Friesiens'.* 'Friedlands! Quelles vaches sont *better for milk?'* That seems to stump his interlocutor – no answer. 'Are you Breton?', he says to somebody. 'No, I'm from Paris.' 'Ah, Paris! *Tray joli.'* Again, I think he's going to pipe down, but no, this time he gets on to Mauritius, which he's going to visit later on. He wants to know about hotels. 'What's better? Luxury or first class?' A woman actually answers him, saying she knows the Île Maurice. My heart sinks. If this goes on, Gary Cooper will have us round the globe. 'Plantations! *Aristocrates? Élégance?'* The woman says there are no big plantations left on Île Maurice. 'No *vie aristocratique?* Sad, sad. No *bon vie?'*

We're coming into Laval.

It's the cue for the irrepressible and inexhaustible Gary to start out on another tack:

'What town is this? How many people? Industry? Intellectual? Nice town! *Beau, joli! Exact'mong. Bon, bon, bon.'*

I think he's maybe finally dried up, and he is in fact silent for a while. But I can feel him back there, casting about in the lone prairie of his mind for something else to say. And it comes. He starts in now about the Musée des Jacobins in Morlaix:

'The Jacobins! Who were the Jacobins??'

Somebody says they were a political party during the Revolution. 'Ah, the Left! Hysterical! Rambouillet! Bang, bang to the king!'

We're approaching Le Mans.

This time, Gary Cooper doesn't talk about the town. But as we roll through the wide plain of the Beauce country, he gets on to wheat: 'Wheat! For Russia to eat! *Oui, nat'rellemong!'* The biggest bore east of

Nebraska, and he has to be on my train. It's not that he's unpleasant; he's just a pain in the neck. But he does shut up for a while – till he sees the name St-Cyr. 'Ah! just like West Point!', he bawls.

By now we're nearing Montparnasse.

Ladies and gentlemen, in a few minutes we will be arriving at Paris-Mont-parnasse. Paris, terminus of this TGV. We hope you have had a pleasant journey. Please make sure you have left nothing on the train. Good-bye, till the next time.

After doing my little Parisian stint, I'm back at Montparnasse station on the Thursday afternoon.

I'm a bit more tired usually than I am when on the way in. Which is why I sometimes buy a newspaper, and after reading it through, doze a little. One time I had taken the evening train I dozed so deeply I woke up just in time to see the noticeboard 'Plouaret-Trégor' disappearing into the night, which meant I had to get out at Morlaix and taxi back to Trébeurden. But that has happened only once.

Memories of Kerouac

A few weeks ago, during one of my Paris trips, somebody gave me a copy of Jack Kerouac's *Satori in Paris*, which I read on my return journey, and which was the occasion for the following pages scribbled in my train notebook.

It's a winter evening, and I'm in the Paris–Brest.

When Kerouac took this train thirty years ago, he said it reminded him of the 'Atlantic line' that went from New York to Richmond, Rocky Mount, Florence, Charleston, Savannah, all the way down to Florida. He was well acquainted with that line, for at the time, while keeping in touch with New York, he was living down there in Florida, at Tampa, alone and reading a lot of French literature: Voltaire's *Candide*, Montherlant's *Un voyageur solitaire est un diable* ('The man who travels alone is a devil'), and Chateaubriand's *Mémoires d'Outre-tombe* ('Memories from beyond the grave'). And a plan was taking shape in his head: to come to France, even to Brittany, in search of his long-lost ancestors, in search too, but it was vaguer in his mind, for something else.

He'd be the first of his family, the first after two hundred years, to go back to source and try and get things clear. He'd come to Brittany, from where the Kerouacs had left for Canada, and thereafter he'd go to Cornwall, and then over to Ireland and up to Scotland, so as to trace the whole line of those unknown characters whose motto had always been: 'Love, suffer, work' – so, also, to get into an as yet unbespoken field.

Jack Kerouac had been a writer, but by now he was a drunkard. Why? Because what he wanted most of all was the mind's ecstasy.

So it wasn't as an artist, even less as a tourist, he was travelling on the Paris-Brest, it was as an old Celtaoist cosmopoetical drunk:

'. . . I just occasionally sip my cognac then go out in the alleyway to look out the window at passing darkness with lights, a lone granite farm-house with lights on just downstairs in the kitchen, and vague hints of hills and moors.'

When he passed through Paris, Kerouac had taken a quick look at the literary scene in the capital. He'd dropped by his French publishers and, while waiting to see the Literary Director, had realised that all the other writers who were also waiting hated his guts. And that was the occasion for Jack The-House-in-the-Field to have a fling at international noveldom seen here in its Parisian avatar:

'. . . this here manuscript called *Silence au Lipp* all about how Renaud walks into the foyer lighting a cigarette and refuses to acknowledge the sad formless smile of the plotless lesbian heroine whose father just died trying to rape an elk in the Battle of Cuckamonga, and Philippe the intellectual enters in the next chapter lighting a cigarette with an existential leap across the blank page . . .'

Kerouac had made his getaway as fast as he could, ultraconscious of the pollution this stuff spreads in the atmosphere.

Over against it, and as far as Cuckamonga, Tallahassee and beyond if need be, Kerouac is ready to defend his own writing practice: the autobiographical saga, the jazzified fiction of the Beat Generation, the swinging automatic writing of the American highway, full of energy and ecstasy as well as a whole lot of other things that the literary clients of the *Brasserie Lipp* have never heard of.

But once he's outside the polemical arena, once he's back in his own head, Jack has doubts also about the kind of literature he himself had produced up tell then.

And that's where old Jack becomes really interesting.

What Kerouac hoped to get from his Euro-Breton escapade was a *satori*, that is, a mental shock, a psychological illumination that would bring about a turning point in his life. If he got to it (from the title of the book, you might think he did, but nowhere do you see it happening, nowhere do you see it taking place – *Satori in Paris* is really the story of a fizzled disappointment), he promised himself he'd start off again in a totally different way.

We'll come back to the story later.

What I want to do now is investigate the kind of thing Jack thought he would write if the desired *satori* did occur, something different from what he'd done before: 'In other words, and after this I'll shut up.' He was fed up to the teeth with the poses and affectations of the Beat Generation, fed up with its palaver and its frenzied rhythm, fed up too with the all the publicity stunts that had gone all around it. He wanted out of all that.

The Breton trip was to be a new departure from a different basis.

So, over there in Florida, he'd carefully prepared this voyage-to-the-end-of-himself, drawing up a programme, deciding on the stages of his itinerary, and it was no doubt of that programme and that itinerary he was thinking as he watched the French landscape flashing by in the train window:

'Studying maps, planning to walk all over, find my ancestors' home town in the library and then go to Brittany where it was and where the sea undoubtedly washed the rocks – My plan being, after five days in Paris, go to that inn on the sea in Finistère and go out at midnight in raincoat, rain hat, with notebook and pencil and with large plastic bag to write inside of, i.e., stick hand, pencil and notebook into bag and write dry, while rain falls on rest of me, write the sounds of the sea, part two of poems "Sea" to be entitled: "SEA, Part Two, the Sounds of the Atlantic at X, Brittany", either at outside of Carnac, or Concarneau, or Pointe de Penmarch, or Douarnenez, or Plouzaimedeau, or Brest, or St Malo . . .'

So, there is the programme: let's say, from history to geography, from millennarism to oceanism, from story-writing to satori-writing . . .

Le Mans.

Rennes.

Saint-Brieuc.

By the time he's got to Saint-Brieuc, Kerouac is already half-seas over: more Jack Cognac than Jack Kerouac. For a part of the way, he'd had a pal to keep him company with drinking and with talking, but from now on he's all alone, and he's beginning to get panicky.

Guingamp.

Plouaret.

Landivisiau.

Landerneau.

Brest, the end of the line.

Once off the train at Brest, Kerouac has the feeling that he's in a strange kind of Nova Scotia. And throughout the following days he's going to wander about like a lost soul in the novascotian nowhere of his mind. He creeps along midnight streets with a paranoiac fear that hordes of savage Finisterrians are getting ready to pounce on him. Or else he stomps up and down the daylight streets, convinced that every gesture he makes is spied upon by 'a lot of little cheap faggots'. The only street that emerges clearly from these misty perambulations is the Rue de Siam, which sparks off in Kerouac's demented brain a vehement protest that he's got nothing to do with Siam, nothing at all: he's not a Buddhist (though God knows he talked about it enough in his Beat books), he's 'a Catholic revisiting the ancestral land'. But Jack is not any kind of pilgrim any more, he's just a lost soul, and he knows it, describing himself as: 'This cowardly Breton (me) watered down by two centuries in Canada and America, nobody's fault but my own, this Kerouac who would be laughed at in Prince of Wales Land because he can't even hunt, or fish, or fight a beef for his fathers, this boastful, this prune, this rage and rake and rack of lacks, "this trunk of humours" as Shakespeare said of Falstaff, this false staff not even a prophet let alone a knight, this fear-of-death tumor, with tumescences in the bathroom, this runaway slave of football fields, this strikeout artist and base thief, this yeller in Paris salons and mum in Breton fogs, this farceur jokester at art galleries of New York . . .'

No need of course to take that at face-value, there's a lot of humour in this semi-masochistic auto-caricature. But the fact is that the whole thing winds down in a sloppy, slobby, back-to-mamma fiasco. Kerouac gives up entirely his idea of continuing his research into Cornwall, Ireland and Scotland. He's homesick. Homesick for America and for Tampa, homesick for home-food. Just plain plum homesick.

So, what is there to say?

That Kerouac's return to Europe was a good idea (the United States, that primal and promised land, is fast going round the bend), but that such an enterprise needs more time, more patience than he was willing or able to give it?

That the kind of literature he was vaguely after remains on the horizon, and that there will be many false prophets, many 'faggots and punks'?

All that, no doubt, and maybe more.

But for the moment, all I'll say is this: 'OK, Jack, you did your best, thanks, *merci* – see you maybe again some day, at some bar in the cosmos, somewhere way up north of Los Angeles. I'll give you the latest news from Armorica, in gull-language.'

BREST, BANGKOK AND THE HUMPBACK WHALE

I'm in the room of a hotel at the bottom of the Rue de Siam, in Brest, beside a window looking out over the Penfeld, the town's river, and the famous old quarter of Recouvrance that seamen have sung about nostalgically all over the world. Of the picturesque port that existed before the bombardments of 1944 little remains. Those bombardments practically wiped Brest off the map. Of course, the town was built up again, in a hurry, but the Brest of Victor Segalen has gone, the Brest of Blaise Cendrars has gone, the Brest of Pierre Mac Orlan has gone, and no doubt the first-year students in the Navy Medical School no longer sing the well-known song about shrivelled foetuses and their future life on the oceans of the world:

> *We are the medic students that nothing can disgust*
> *And whom the town of Brest has welcomed to its breast*
> *Before the hungry ocean swallows us all up*
> *Let us altogether merrily sing and wine and sup*
>
> *We are the little foetuses*
> *The very little foetuses*
> *The abortive little foetuses*
> *Steeped in alcohol*
> *We are the wee wee foetuses*
> *The teeny weeny foetuses*
> *All shrinkled and contorted*
> *From head to arse-hole*

Well, the end of an old song can mean the beginning of a new map. And that can sometimes mean going back beyond the old into the very old, and out into uncharted territory . . .

As everybody knows, well, nearly everybody, the Rue de Siam was named after the Siamese embassy to France (three ambassadors, six mandarins wearing conical hats with rings round the rim according to rank, and interpreters, and secretaries and servants and guards) in the month of June 1686. But what everybody maybe doesn't know was what lay behind that embassy, as well as the one that preceded it (but didn't pass through Brest) in 1683.

To get it all in place, you have to move from the Rade de Brest to the Bay of Bengal, making the acquaintance there of a Greek called Constant Phaulkon and an Englishman by the name of Samuel White, the latter an adventurer, the former a visionary.

Let me tell the story. I know it quite well, since, several years back now, I actually picked up the tracks of White in Thailand.

By 1670, Sam White's brother, George, was out in Madras as a free merchant, that is, working outside the framework of the East India Company, though sometimes collaborating with some of its functionaries. At that time, the climate being what it was, 'somewhat sulphureous', as a seventeenth-century text puts it, and the whole environment malaria-ridden, so that a residence of ten years would turn you into a total wreck, the idea, if you could, was to make your pile as fast as possible and hurry back home, to become a gentleman of leisure and a pillar of the community – like, say, the American Elihu Yale who was out there for a while at this time before going back home and founding a university. George was doing good business, which is one reason why Sam followed him out there to the Orient of dangers and delights with a job as pilot attached to Fort St George, Madras, the headquarters of the East India Company. It was there he met for the first time Constant Phaulkon, who was George's assistant. Sam had desires. Constant had both desires and ideas.

In no time at all, Phaulkon was at Ayudhya, the capital of Siam, and Sam was at Mergui, Siam's outpost on the Bay of Bengal. And they were both making it, in all kinds of ways.

At Ayudhya, where King Phra Narai lived surrounded by mandarins and astrologers when he wasn't out on safari trips looking for white elephants, Phaulkon quickly became a mandarin of the third class and head of the department of foreign trade, before turning almost as quickly, not only into a mandarin of the first class, but Prime Minister. Phra Narai's Siam, Constant Phaulkon knew, was neither Aurangzebe's India nor K'ang Hsi's China, but as the go-between of those empires, it had a future both economical and political. Phaulkon was well aware he could expect nothing from the mandarins, and that he would never be able to work with them, which was why he kept Sam White as his right-hand man.

The waters of the Bay of Bengal were infested with pirates and philibusters and its Siamese coast was rife with beachcombers from Portugal, Holland, England and France, ready for anything. Sam had an eye to everything. His house, complete with warehouse, stood fifty feet above a private wharf, and from his window he had a control-tower lookout on to the Mergui harbour as well as a sea-view out to the island of Pataw. Phaulkon had got him nominated as *shahbandar* of the port, which meant chief commissioner for Siamese maritime affairs in the Bay of Bengal, and had offered him subsequently an even higher position at Ayudhya. But Sam, wily man, felt it was safer to be out on the coast, with a ship riding at anchor, ready for a fast getaway, because you never know.

With projects of expansion in mind, Phaulkon had made overtures to the English East India Company, but John Company was out only for profit and wanted no political complications. Which was why Phaulkon turned to the French. Up to now, they had only been doing missionary work, but Phaulkon soon got them interested in his political and economic plans.

It was he who engineered the Siamese embassy to France in 1683, the French embassy to Siam in 1685, and the subsequent Siamese embassy to France in 1686.

All might have been well. France might have made a lasting deal with Thailand. And Brest might have been second cousin to Bangkok. But disaster came in 1688, with the mandarins of Ayudhya, whom Phaulkon had dismissed as too ignorant and retrograde, wanting to get their own back. They flung Phaulkon into prison, had him tortured, then executed. His wife, who was Japanese, went through torture too before being appointed to a cake-walk position as Controller of the Royal Confectionery. As to Sam White, he managed to beat it back to England with a quarter of a million quid to his credit, but he died, shaking with malaria, before he could make use of it.

So much for history. Now let's get down into the street. As aforesaid, the picturesqueness is gone. The old stone and wood has disappeared, cement and metal taking their place. You won't see, at the exit from some seamy den, Loulou the bighearted joy girl hanging on to the arms of two red-pommed sailorboys and a wheezy accordeon playing in the background, but you will see some goodlooking Brestoises breasting the breeze. And there are still some oriental vestiges.

There's that spicy capharnaum, for example, where you can buy all kinds of exotic produce from plum pudding to Korean ginseng, passing through Moskovskaya vodka, caviar from Iran and fresh vanilla from the island of Reunion. I'd stopped at the window one afternoon and was quietly reading a Chinese poem about tea ('The first cup refreshes my lips and throat; the second cup breaks my solitude; the third goes down into my insides and sets a thousand strange ideograms dancing; the fourth provokes a slight sweat, and all the badness of my life disappears through my pores; at the fifth cup, I am purified; the sixth carries me to the realm of the immortals; with the seventh, ah, the seventh, I feel an icy wind blowing up my sleeves . . .') when a guy leapt out of the shop and snap-shotted me. Before the door closed again, I had time to hear someone say: 'He's right – maybe that fellow's out to smash his window.' The owner must have thought I was casing the joint. In fact, I was on the point of going in with the firm intention (a notice in the window: 'Loiterers aren't welcome!' made it clear that you went into that shop with firm intentions, or else) of buying some tea, and maybe some vodka (I imagined myself having a transcendental little snort at the window of my hotel maybe around midnight), but passed on – the guy might have come at me this time with a kalachnikov.

To get into what used to be the old romantic quarter of Brest, Recouvrance, you pass over a bridge across the Penfeld, at the bottom of the Rue de Siam. All around, blue cranes, a huddle of grim military-grey boats, and ship's horns sounding near and far.

Wandering round the streets there, on either side the Rue de la Porte, I didn't find the bar *Chez Olga*, which existed here years ago, when I first visited Brest as a student of French language and life, and I saw that *Le Cabanon*, a restaurant in the Rue du Quartier-Maître Boudon, had closed down, though you could still read the information 'From 7pm till dawn' painted on the wall.

I came back down to the Rue de la Porte that moves off in the direction of Le Conquet, where you take the boat for the seal-rocked, dolphin-haunted waters of Molène and Ouessant.

It's midnight now.

When I said of the waters of Molène and Ouessant that they were 'dolphin-haunted', I wasn't just being gratuitously poetic. It's one of the phenomena of these recent years: the presence, along the Atlantic coast, from the sea of Iroise up to the Scottish archipelagoes, not only of grey seals, but of bands of dolphins, usually small bands of about five or six individuals, but sometimes larger, maybe up to a hundred.

I'm thinking of those dolphins. And of whales, the biggest migrants of the Atlantic, either keeping close to the continental plateau and the coast, or moving farther out, feeding in cold waters, reproducing in warmer. I'm hearing the cry of the humpback, but also the cry of the nomad orca off the Pacific coast of Canada and, away in the distance, the plaintive cries of the antarctic orca in the Crozet archipelago . . .

All this turns into a kind of abstraction, full of fish and mammals and meteorological movement.

And maybe that's what Brest represents for me now. Not a pleasure harbour, not a commercial harbour, not a naval arsenal, not picturesqueness and nostalgia, but a place of live thought, a point of departure for migratory ideas . . .

September on Ushant

I t's a September evening in Brest. I'm in a room at a hotel at the top of the Rue de Siam, which, in a glass cabinet in the foyer, has a display of old marine objects, two of which particularly attracted my attention when I came in: a Borda *cercle de réflexion* and an eighteenth-century Neptune map of the Atlantic. I've just had dinner in the hotel's restaurant. At the table next to me three women on in years but very lively (a bottle of red-glowing Bordeaux helped them along) were talking about their dead husbands and their living dogs. I was thinking of Ushant, out there at the limit of the Channel, in the Sea of the Iroise, that area of rock, mist, changing light, wind and fast currents like that of the Fromveur (Breton for 'the great fear'). The name Ushant itself is supposed to be old Celtic, from an adjective *ux* meaning 'high' and a superlative *sama*, so that it means 'the highest island'. Not that Ushant is very high, but it is high compared with the flat islands of the Molène archipelago. When Pytheas, the navigator from the then Greek port of Marseilles, sailed by here in the fourth century BC before reconnoitering the mainland capes of the *Ostidamnii* ('the sunset people') and continuing his way up north, he transcribed the island's name as *Uxisama*. Later Greek navigators, geographers and naturalists were to call it *Axantos* (Pliny the Ancient) and *Uxantisima* (Ptolemy). In the Latin of the fourth century AD, it was *Uxantis*, which is next door to Ushant . . .

It's the beginning of an extraordinary beautiful day as I walk along the Rue de Siam at half past seven the next morning. I come down the Rue de Siam, then turn left into the Rue Traverse and continue on along there till I reach the Rue de Denver near the imposing monument raised by the U.S. of America after the Second World War (not far from it, discreetly set in a wall, a plaque commemorating the departures of Rochambeau and De Grasse from Brest to aid the Americans during the War of Independence). I then go down the steps, cross the rusty old railway track, making for the offices of the *Penn-Ar-Bed* ('Finisterrian') shipping company. Ticket in pocket, I stroll thereafter around the harbour waiting for the departure of the *Enez Eussa* ('*Isle of Ushant*') III, which makes the island trip every day, blow, rain or shine, and which is at present loading cargo. A red sun is moving up a rosy sky, almost following the angle of the cranes. Those sturdy little boats called *abeilles* ('bees') are moving out for a busy day in the Brest roadstead.

The *Enez Eussa* foams along at a good rate. We pass by the naval base of the Western Squadron (*l'Escadre du Ponant*) with its line of ancient anchors hooked over the jetty. Spurts of harpy and fluty Celtic music come over the loudspeaker, but you can't get hold of it for the throb and thud of the engine. What you do hear clearly is the occasional piercing cry of a gull. There's a blue haze over the water that appears now smoky now frosty. A huge petrol tanker, rust-red below, black above, looms out of the blue morning towards us. We passed Spanish Point some time back, now we're approaching St Matthew's Point with its ruins of a benedictine monastery (The Church at the World's End) and its lighthouse. The next thing to attract my attention is the red beacon Les Renards – on it are perched five cormorants. Then, after a stop at Le Conquet, we're out into the open, moving steadily north-west.

At one time, the Armorican promontory stretched even farther west than it does now. Then (how many million years ago?), due to ice melting, the sea-level rose and a lot of land was flooded. What's left is a cluster of spurs, crags, stacks, skerries and little plateaux. That's the Molène archipelago. What the eye sees in the now clear-blue crystal light of this September morning are scores of stony islets, and the sea tossing whitely around them. In the distance, a vague line that is the sand beach of some bigger island. Down there towards the south, the long ragged reef of the Black Rocks. Over there, Kervouroc, then Beniguet, and the Kemenez group, and the Enez ar C'hriszienn ('the Christians' island') . . . We turn round the lighthouse of the Three Stones, pass the marker Bazou Real and make for the harbour of Molène (*moal enez*, the bald or bare island?), our next port of call. After Molène, more rocks, islands, skerries: Balanec, Bannec, till Ushant comes in sight across the Fromveur, a longish mass rising up gradually in a straight line from south-west to north-east.

At Stiff harbour, on Ushant's east side, a taxi driven by a burly bloke, with a curly black beard and a big piratical ring in his ear, takes me to the island's town, Lampaul. There I get myself a room at a little hotel (the door to my room has a porthole with a curtain over it) and lay out my things before taking a stroll. I end up making for a nice-looking pancake-house I'd noticed in the bygoing. It turns out this used to be the only inn and hostelry on the island, frequented by all the ghoul-hunters of the nineteenth century, I mean all those who went around the country districts gathering stories, legends and superstitions, thinking they were 'saving the soul of the people' and contributing to world culture. It's this kind of stuff you still find in the local bookshops, alongside a host of novels about tempest, terror and tears, not to speak of pig-slaughtering (the ethno-boys delight in this kind of thing). I was to meet up with more than one Ushanter who was fed up with it all. The island wants to move over into something else. What that 'something else' is may not be represented by the meal I saw offered on a tourist menu called the TGV (I liked the humour of it): an American ham-filled sandwich, followed by a piece of *far* (a traditional Breton cake), followed by an Italian *espresso*. But it's what Ushant, and other places like it, *could* mean. A place devoted to a certain sense of life.

There's a whole network of footpaths running all round Ushant. Already on the boat I'd read a notice asking visitors to respect them and not to use even bikes on them. When I saw the number of mountain-bikes for hire at Lampaul, I had the feeling that the bike-hirers would not be very likely to encourage this respect. But who knows? There's plenty of biking can be done on the island's roads, so maybe the paths can be left to animals and birds and plants and meditative wanderers. Anyway, it was with this hope in mind that I set out from Lampaul for a walk along the Loc Gweltas peninsula to the west of the island.

The rocks are amazing. Brittany is full of strangely shaped rocks, of gneiss, schist and granite, but never have I seen craggier, crazier forms than here on Ushant. To walk along the coastline is to see one grotesque rock gesture after another. On the spurs and pinnacles, gulls of many kinds (common gulls, laughing gulls, herring gulls, great black-headed gulls), and, flying low over the sea-moor with its clumps of purple heather and its beds of silver-faded *armeria*, red-beaked choughs. I move along the edge of creek after creek till I come to the tip of the Pointe de Pern, when I turn north, up to the Creac'h lighthouse, one of the most powerful in the world, that attracts birds migrating from the British isles and the continent of Europe, at times offering a welcome rest, at others delivering sudden death. At the lighthouse museum close by, I'm interested particularly in a map of the Roman lighthouses, all the way from the Adriatic to the British Channel. It seems a thorough piece of work, like everything else in the museum (except the 'art work', sculptures and paintings, that some well-meaning local 'representative of culture' has thought fit to display) – but away up by the Black Sea some expert in lighthouses or in Roman civilisation has pencilled in one that's been omitted: Tanaïs.

Outside again, I keep on walking in a north-easterly direction, passing a tethered sheep here and there, beaches piled with boulders, pools packed with jungles of laminarian seaweed, till I come to the Bay of Beninou. There I start back to Lampaul, making only a little detour to visit an example of the old island house. These houses were divided, usually by a barrier of cupboards, into the 'ashen end' (*penn lous*), the kitchen area, and the 'fine end' (*penn brao*), the reception area. Since there are no trees on the island, apart from small willows in the softer, wetter middle valley, most of the wooden structures come from flotsam and jetsam.

When I awake the next morning and take a still half-somnolent look out the window down into the back garden of my inn, I wonder if I'm not in the Tropics. Ushant may have been called 'the garden of storms' (*jardin ar gwall-amzer*) but down there in that little garden there's a flowering century plant. And it's another splendid Indian summer day. After a quick breakfast, I set out for another peninsula, the south-

western one, Feunteun Velen. Yesterday I did come across the occasional group of helter-skelter bikers on the coastal path, but this
morning, no doubt because it's still too early, I don't meet a soul,
pedalling or otherwise, only gulls, either marshalled on the beach all
facing the sun, or else niched in solitude here and there, and crows,
foraging in thick piles of seaweed. In the distance, now and then,
swarms of little birds, no doubt migrators on their way to some warm
south for the winter. Again, wild-shaped rocks, frequently white-
beshitten, and the path leading through heather (dark-red *erica* and
the paler pink *calluna*), bramble, fern, sloe-bushes and honeysuckle.
This south-south-west part of the island was the one that saw the most
shipwrecks, as a report written on the island in 1681 puts it: *'Le bout de
l'isle Doüessant le plus exposé au mauvais temps est celuy d'Oüest Suroüest et c'est sur
ce bout que se font presque tous les nauffrages.'* It's the area past which that wild
sea-river, the Fromveur, courses. Wherever you turn your eyes, you see
a lighthouse. I come along by Penn ar Roc'h and make my way up to
Penn Arland by Bouge an Dour, Porz Gwenn and Penn ar C'hreac'h.
Everywhere, sun glinting on mica, here and there, clumps of wild
carrot or *criste marine* and, once, in a quiet creek, and the blue-green
water lapping against the rocks, a white heron.

I spent a week there on Ushant (it seemed to get quieter with every
passing day), in the company of stones, plants and birds: a prolonged
silence interspersed with only a few minimal conversations. One man
about fifty years old told me that in the summer months the island
was hellish, with six or more boats of tourists coming in every day,
and that I'd been right to come in September. Given this annual
invasion, I hardly dare think what will become of Ushant. One has an
awful fleeting vision of amusement parks, motor-bike races and
casinos. When St Pol Aurelian and St Gildas set foot on it and
started raising crosses, if they experienced the kind of Indian summer
weather I did, they must have thought it was Paradise. I wouldn't talk
about Paradise, at least not too loudly (people talk about it, then do

everything they can to make anything like it impossible), all I can say is that these September days spent on Ushant, the time of a first reconnaissance, will stay in my mind like pages of sun, earth, sea and wind in a bible of the biosphere.

Season's End
at Huelgoat

In the graveyard at Huelgoat, there's a great recumbent slab of crude granite, on which is inscribed, in large, boldly-cut, black letters, this information: VICTOR SEGALEN 14 JAN. 1878–21 MAI 1919. Away at the bottom of the stone, there is also a small cross and the word PAX. Beside the stone grows a little oak tree. All around spreads the forest of Huelgoat, at the centre of the land's end district of Brittany . . .

It was a day at the end of September, with a blue sky full of grey-and-white cloud. It could have turned to rain, but it didn't. What the day offered was an alternating play of light and shadow, the autumn sun now visible, now hidden.

From Gwenved, you get out on to the Trébeurden–Lannion road. At Lannion, you cross the Pont de Viarmes and make up the hill for the road to Plestin-les-Grèves.

Passing Locquémeau on the right, I'm thinking of an antique and curiosity shop I like to browse about in down by its harbour. I've bought all kinds of things in that shop: a tray from a Japanese tea-house, an old Dutch wine decanter, a bamboo brush-holder from China My last purchase was a treatise on meteorology, with a long section on clouds: *Nuages, types de ciels, systèmes nuageux*, and with a whole series of plates representing *cumulus humilis, cumulus congestus, cumulus pileus, cumulonimbus calvus, cumulonimbus incus, stratocumulus vesperalis, stratocumulus cumulogenitus, stratocumulus translucidus, stratocumulus opacus, altostratus translucidus, altrostratus opacus, altocumulus translucidus, altocumulus lenticularis, altocumulus opacus, cirrus filosus, cirrus densus, cirrostratus nebulosus* . . .

By the time that cloudy paragraph has crossed the sky of your mind, we'll have reached Saint-Michel-en-Grève and be interested in more human details, such as the gestures of the people walking around the *Hôtel de la Plage* and gazing out over the long, seaweed-scattered beach towards the line of rollers lit by the autumn sun.

After St-Efflam and the Big Rock, we bump over the cobbles of the centre of Plestin, past the fine-looking church, past the Town Hall with its modern front of blue tubes and glass, past the Municipal Culture Bureau (*Ti an oll*), getting out on to the road to Gremel, with Morlaix over there to the west shining like a bed of oysters.

We're following a clean little, quiet little departmental road (the D 42), bordered by maize-fields and ferny-heathery moorland, with here and there scattered willow, oak and rowan, or a field with rolls of harvested hay. Already we see the needle-steeple of Plouégat-Moysan (i.e. *Plegad Moezan*). Then it's Guerlesquin (*Gwirliskin*), another lovely little Breton town, with a fine square surrounded by solid, beautiful houses, which some nitwit has thought fit to 'embellish' with what could enter a competition for the ugliest and silliest fountain in Europe, a contraption in glass, painted with bands of seven colours, and with three curved tubes, meant, one assumes, to represent a rainbow. Will some mayor of the future have the courage to get rid of it? At Scrignac (*Skrigneg*), we leave the Côtes-d'Armor (*Aodou an Arvor*) and enter the Finistère (*Penn ar Bed*). After Berrien, we're on the last short lap to Huelgoat, seeing a hawk on the hover and a herd of white cattle grazing in a field with that resignation and fatalism of animals that many a human on the edge of humanity has admired and even envied.

And here's Huelgoat on a late September afternoon, at the far end of the century.

An agreeable little grey granite town, in one of the most beautiful and interesting sites in Brittany, Huelgoat has its share of visitors from many countries. Witness the number of cars with British and German licence plates parked along the lakeside (I notice one in particular, with a sticker: 'Scottish Idea – Alba'), and the amount of publications in several languages (*Der Spiegel, The Guardian, La Repubblica, De Telegraaf, Algemeen Dagblad, The European*) stocked by the local newsagent. Yet there is an air of abandonment about the place, and it's not only because it's a season's ending. The *Hôtel de Bretagne* is up for sale, and it doesn't take me long to see that there are 'For Sale' notices on at least a dozen other good-looking houses. I am glad to see that the *Crêperie des Myrtilles*, a hunched stony little den, is still there and still open, though hardly doing a thriving business at this particular moment – as we pass, I see only one woman, maybe the owner, with a cigarette dangling from her lips, playing patience. We then pass the *Art Breton* shop, stacked up with plates, jugs and soup turreens from the Quimper crockery-factories (not the most exciting thing in

Christendom), and go into the church, just in case there is something interesting. There isn't: only a trio of painted wooden statues to the left of the choir representing the parish saint of the town, Saint-Yves, flanked by a rich man and a poor man. And yet maybe there is: I watch the redorange flicker on the grey granite as the sun shines through the plate-glass windows, listening to the ponderous *tick-tock, tick-tock* of the clock . . .

Coming out of the church with the intention of making for the forest, we walk down the Rue des Cendres, and there is an old, familiar smell in the air: somebody is cooking jam. It is as if the wood smoke drifting from the chimneys had bramble juice mixed in with it.

It's maybe the thought of jam (who can be aware of all the connections?) that makes us decide to pay a visit to a honey-factory, a *miellerie*, we saw signposted. The building turns out to be what, when I first visited Huelgoat years ago, was a clog-maker's shop: in memory of it, a line of clogs is laid out along a bench. Even at that time, the old man only made souvenir clogs for decorative purposes, but he continued the job up to the late 1980s when, I learn, the place was taken over by his grandson, a bee-keeper. The counter is piled up with pots of honey: heather honey, colza honey, buckwheat honey, and opposite it, a tray of bees is busily at work, with hundreds of brown drones swarming round a queen one and a half times their size.

There are boulders scattered throughout the forest of Huelgoat, huge moss-covered lumps, and sometimes split, the way granite often splits, but there's a concentration of them there at the forest's entrance, on the edge of town. They've been giving various pictur-esque, imaginative names: the *Grotte du Diable*('the devil's grotto'), the *Ménage de la Vierge*('the Virgin's kitchen'), but the ground term, the operative term is *chaos*. It's in that sense of chaos that the poetry lies, and it's geological poetry.

After the chaos, we start following out the paths – these that skirt the river, and those that lead away from it up to the plateau from where you get a panorama of all the surrounding countryside: the Monts d'Arrée in the north and west, the Forêt de Gréau and the Montagnes Noires in the east and south.

Beech, oak and pine, their roots veining the earth. Sunlight on the brown waters of the river, and skelter-insects making circles on their surface. Mica sparkling in granite. The little thud as another acorn falls. The mauve of heather. The extraordinary red of a bramble leaf. A bird swooping along the river, and others, invisible: *phweet, phweet; tseu, tseu, tseu, tseu.*

Around six, the wind grows stronger. Retracing our steps, we go back into town and sit in the *Café du Chaos*, drinking a coffee, listening to the conversation between the proprietrix and two men drinking wine at the counter:

'The sky was clearer today.'

'It was chilly this morning.'

'You could see the houses in the lake; it was like a mirror.'

'I was thinking to myself that if the weather was going to be fine, it would be really hot.'

'Oh, you never can tell, the clouds were creeping up, you can never be sure.'

Leaving the square Aristide-Briand, we stand at the crossroads where the Rue des Cieux leads up to the chapel of the same name and the cemetery, and where the Rue du Docteur-Jacq, which is part of the D 764 to Carhaix, leads to the Gouffre, where the Silver River runs underground for a hundred yards or so. A flight of steps runs down from the road to where two white-satin sashes of water plunge down with a roar over the black-gleaming rocks.

On the other side of the river, a path leads up the hill, runs past a rockface covered with lichen, till it comes to a copse of beech and oak. In that copse stands a stela, a slab of rough granite, at its centre a smooth dark plaque on which is written, in golden letters, this:

VICTOR SEGALEN

1878–1919

BORN IN BREST

NAVY DOCTOR

POET AND WRITER

DIED HERE

21 MAY 1919

It was on this spot exactly that, on 23rd May 1919, the body of Victor Segalen was found lying at the foot of a tree, with a copy of *Hamlet* at his side. This site in the forest of Huelgoat marks the end of a life devoted to a radical kind of poetic research.

Segalen's life-search was for a fundamental otherness. It's everyone's desire to 'get outside one's self', but here it was pursued with greater determination and pushed to its furthest limits. The poet Arthur Rimbaud had cried: '*Je est un autre*' (the self is an other). He had tried to get at that 'other' by mental processes (among them, what he called 'the deregulation of all the senses'), laying them out in books such as *A Season in Hell* and *The Illuminations*, then by a geographical displacement, moving finally to the Somali desert, where, among other activities, he explored unknown regions of the Ogadine, sending back a report to the Geographical Society in Paris, and dying, at the age of 37, in a Marseilles hospital. Segalen tries to pick up where Rimbaud left off. He studies the poet, he studies the explorer, and by a kind of triangulation, he imagines a third figure, outside 'poet' and 'explorer', raising them both to a higher unity, which, using a neologism of his invention, he calls the *exote*. For Segalen, as he says in his *Essays on Exotism* (left incomplete in a fragmentary state, like so much of his work), the syllable 'exo' indicates 'all that's outside the context of our ordinary, daily consciousness, all that lies beyond our habitual tonality'. The fulfilment of the exote's desire will mean at least partly the moving through foreign countries, exotic territories – Segalen's own life-itinerary was to take him from Brest to Polynesia, China and the frontiers of Tibet. But this movement meant much more than superficial exoticism or ethnological documentation. If Segalen is 'an inspector of races, an observer of places' (as he says in his *Journal des Îles*), if he is out to maintain differences (he calls that 'the aesthetics of difference') and deplores a uniformisation process he sees taking place all over the world, the 'exotic', the 'otherness' he is after goes beyond local colour, local costume, local custom. He says (in the *Journal des Îles*) that he wants his 'exotic' to be *pure*, 'cleared of absurdities and excrescences'. And one needs only read his essay on Gauguin, superficially much more 'exotic' than he was himself, to see how far he is from the 'human science' of ethnology. With regard to exotic communities, foreign groups, he says the thing is 'to imagine more than one knows, to think in their place, to see with their eyes, to tell things in their way, say what they might have said'. All this means that the self has to be supple enough to feel its way into all kinds of diverse fields, and still retain the energy required to penetrate into *a farther field*. While painting his Polynesian pictures, making use of exotic mythology, Gauguin certainly never forgot what he had once said himself: that what he really wanted to get on to his canvases was the sound his clogs made on granite ground. And it was a similarly fundamental tonality that Segalen was after. Polynesia had meant for him an enlargement of the self via an extension of the senses. China was less extension than intention: the tendency to penetrate into the centre of the centre of the centre (where in the Forbidden City, the Empress sat like a queen bee . . .). I imagine that in the forest of Huelgoat it was this fundamental tonality he had in mind.

Segalen had left China in July 1917, going from Peking to Hong-Kong and from Hong-Kong to Hanoi. Off Singapore, the steamer he was travelling on had an accident, which meant that he was holed up in Singapore for over a month – he used the time to work at his long poem, *Thibet*. By the beginning of March 1918, he was in Marseilles. In May and July, he was undergoing training at the Hôpital Saint-Louis in Paris for a post he was to occupy (he was still a navy doctor) at Brest. That autumn he was working overtime at a navy hospital there in Brest. By mid-November, he was exhausted, and had to stop. He felt weaker and weaker, fell seriously ill in January, and was hospitalised at the Val-de-Grâce, the military hospital, in Paris. Thereafter he was sent to Algeria for convalescence. But there was little improvement in his general condition. In April, he wrote to a friend: 'I don't know what's wrong with me. I have no known disease [. . .] I just feel that life is leaving me.' During those months, April and May, he was at Huelgoat, taking daily walks in the forest, speaking in a letter to his wife about 'a labour of patience'. On the morning of 21 May, a Wednesday, he left the *Hôtel d'Angleterre* with a cold snack and a copy of *Hamlet*, intending to spend another day in the woods. He was never seen alive again.

We can only imagine what went on in his mind, what kind of strange delirium took place during those last vague moments in the forest.

To start with, there would have been Hamlet's famous question 'to be or not to be' – with Segalen maybe thinking (I am putting myself momentarily in his skin) that the question is really not 'to be or not to be' but 'to be *and* not to be' There would be clouds in the sky, as often in Brittany, and he would think of the dialogue with Polonius in which Hamlet describes a cloud as like a camel, then as like a weasel, then as like a whale, with Polonius, taking him for a madman to be humoured, agreeing wholeheartedly all the time: 'very like a whale' – in fact, very like the big belly of China, or the snowy summits of the land of Bod. Clouds and rocks, clouds and rocks What more exotic, more definitely and rockily other, than granite? Maybe after *Thibet* he would write the book of granite, with some old Breton playing the role that the Tahitians had played in *Les Immémoriaux*, an image of the self. The self and the drama of history, the self and the dream of being.

We stayed an hour or so up by the stela. When we got back down on the public road, it was to see that the clouds had cleared and that the sky was all blue.

It was blue, of that bright nirvana blue, all the way back to Gwenved.

AT THE HOSPITAL

If it hadn't been for those three yards of mail laid side up along the floor, maybe I wouldn't have broken my toe.

I'd just come back from a few weeks' absence, and there was all that mail waiting for me. In order to see my way through it easier, as I thought, I'd converted the pile into a line. But that line changed my habitual trajectory. Making my way from the kitchen towards the staircase that leads to the bedroom, I had to skirt round the mail-ridge, which meant I was nearer than usual to the corner of the staircase. Which was how, barefoot, I came to stub my toe on the edge of the staircase, and stub it hard. Not only did I feel an intense pain, but looking down, I was aghast to see that the little toe of my right foot was hanging limp, at an angle of 90° from its normal position. When she'd heard me howl, Marie-Claude had said: 'What's up?!' When I told her I'd broken my toe, she said 'No, you've only hurt it, that's always very painful.' I said 'No, it's broken, really broken, look at it.' When she saw me tenderly and precautiously propping the toe upright, and then watching it flop back into its abnormal position, she couldn't help laughing. And I laughed too. But I really felt like crying. That was my dear little toe down there, that had done me such good service, without ever really being noticed or appreciated, and there it was looking utterly useless and forlorn.

Marie-Claude phoned up the *Urgences* at Lannion hospital while I very gingerly put on a pair of thick socks. It was half past nine at night. At the hospital, they put me into a wheelchair, left me waiting a little while, then wheeled me to the X-ray. Yes, my toe was well and truly bust, and pretty badly at that. I'd have to see the doctor-surgeon as fast as possible. I said I had to leave early the next morning for Grenoble (where I had a talk to do). So we made the appointment for three days' time. In the meantime, the nurse taped up my foot. She told me they didn't plaster up injuries like this any more, for the plaster often did more harm than good, they just spliced the broken toe to the one next to it . . .

After that, Marie-Claude and I went over to the chemist's shop to buy some pain-killer pills, just in case, and hire a couple of crutches, of the kind called *cannes anglaises* ('English sticks').

And so I hirpled down to Grenoble on my English sticks, gave my talk, and hirpled back up again to Trébeurden.

Three days later, I'm up at Lannion hospital (in Breton they say: *ospital*) to see the surgeon.

After quite a while, I'm told I have to go the radiography and am given a paper. I go to the *radiographie-scanner*, slide my paper through a slit in the glass partition separating me from a nurse at a counter, wait another while, till she tells me to go and sit down and wait there.

I wait.

After about five minutes, a guy comes swinging in on crutches, Long John Silver kind of character, old hand at the game, swings up to the glass partition, slips in his paper, sits down, and in no time at all is called to the radiography unit.

I think maybe he's a special case, and keep on patiently waiting.

But then an older man comes in, slips his paper in to the nurse, sits down, and, hey presto, he also is called right away.

By now, I am convinced there is something unusual going on.

I go over to the counter.

'Yes?'

'I came for a radiography.'

'Your paper.'

I just look at her.

'Your paper. Give me your paper.'

'I gave you my paper half an hour ago.'

She looks bewildered, searches around, finds my paper lying at the end of the desk.

'What's that paper doing there?!' she cries.

'Can we pick up from there?' I say.

'I'll ring the radiography people.'

I see her ringing them up.

Nobody appears. Nothing happens.

She finally takes the paper through herself.

A couple of minutes later, I'm called, and get rayed.

I then go for my appointment with the surgeon, Dr Marquet. While he's examining my radiography, he says:

'Aren't you a singer?'

I say: 'No, I'm not a singer.'

'Well,' he says, 'there's a singer with your name.'

I ask him how long it's going to be before my toe's mended.

'About six weeks,' he says.

'Six weeks!'

'Some people are in plaster for three months,' he says.

So I'm to consider myself lucky.

All I've got to do is wait – it'll mend itself. Banal case. People are always breaking their toes. Very banal case.

I keep hirpling about the world which suddenly seems a whole lot bigger.

After about ten days, my toe has swollen up, red and hard. I phone up the hospital. They fix an appointment

I'm waiting on the chairs outside the Surgery and Dressing rooms. Time goes by. An old man beside me says: 'Time stops here.' And an old woman next to him says: 'And there's no respect for people.' I just shrug. I can always see several sides to a question.

There's a sheet lying on a desk. A list of names. I check to see if my name is on it. It is. But there's still nobody around. Then I see a man in a white coat passing, waylay him, and say:

'I just wanted to make sure I was on the list.'

'You waiting for the surgeon?'

'Yes.'

'You better go to the radiography.'

I go to the radiography.

'The last time I was here', I say to the girl through the glass window, 'you lost me.'

She laughs.

This time I'm called almost right away.

When I pass again in front of the guichet, the girl says:

'OK this time?'

'Great,' I say.

I then go back over to External Consultations. There's a long queue.

My turn comes eventually. A nurse ushers me in to a room, briskly cuts off the dressing, and rejoins her colleagues in a room adjoining, leaving me for the surgeon's inspection. I hear her saying to the other nurses: 'It's the artist.'

In comes Dr Marquet.

He takes a good look at the X-ray and my toe, and pronounces the fatal words:

'It's stewing in its juice.'

He calls in a nurse, and says:

'No dressing.'

'But', I say, 'my toe isn't in the right position.'

'We'll see in three weeks,' he says.

'But it'll have had time to set at a tangent!'

'It's stewing,' he says. 'We've got to give it air. No dressing.'

OK, he's the boss.

I ask if I should go on walking normally, or rest up.

'Walk', he says, 'according to the pain.'

I say that, if need be, I mean if it's *good* to walk, I can stand quite a lot of pain. So how do I know when to stop?

'Just play it by ear,' he says.

So I continue to limp about, sometimes quite painfully. I have things to do in Paris, in Brest, in Bordeaux . . . My little toe is still swollen and red, and inflammation seems to be spreading up my foot. Now and then, I go down to the Pors Mabo beach, paddle in the water, and hopefully wrap my foot in seaweed. But the swelling doesn't go down.

When, at the next hospital appointment, I go, with my X-ray, to see the surgeon, he says:

'It's developed an abcess. The bone's all mashed up. We'll have to operate.'

Half-stunned, half-relieved, I follow instructions. I am to report the next morning, 24 April, at the hospital, with nothing in my stomach. In the meantime, I am to go upstairs and see the anaesthetist.

I go upstairs, tell the nurse at a desk I am to see the anaesthetist.

She checks, and ushers me into a room with two beds, telling me to undress, put on the white shirt she takes out of a cupboard for me, and get into the bed by the window. There is nobody in the other bed, but the TV set on the wall is flickering greyly . . .

In comes the anaesthetist, who asks me a few questions and takes my pulse.

I say:

'It'll be a local anaesthetic, I suppose?

'No,' he says, 'it'll be an *agé* (a general anaesthesia), because if we injected liquid, there'd be a danger of spreading the pus. But don't worry, everything's going to be all right. There'll be no after-effects. Just don't sign any cheques right away . . .'

It's a strange evening Marie-Claude and I spend at Gwenved. Sure, the operation isn't a major one. But I've never been operated on in my life. And neither of us likes the idea of a general anaesthesia. I mean, you can conk out during those things. And did I give the anaesthetist the necessary information? Suddenly Marie-Claude remembers an electrocardiogram made some years ago. She delves into a drawer and brings it out. I'm not to forget to show it to the anaesthetist the next day.

We're up at seven, and by eight sharp we're at the hospital. I am allotted a bed, and given one of those white shirts that fasten at the back. I'm told the surgeon is alone today in the hospital, the other two being on holiday. So they have no idea when he'll be able to take me on.

I lie in bed, hearing distant sounds of TV or radio. Fortunately, nothing in this room. What I do hear in the immediate vicinity is the heavy breathing and occasional snoring of my neighbour. And I can smell the stale guff coming from the stubs of cigarettes in the ashtray. Outside, there's a beautiful blue April sky, the bright yellow of whin, lines of white-walled houses, crows flying over the white, the blue, and the yellow, and a black dog loping and sniffing along the road. I really envy that dog.

My neighbour goes into a horrible series of snorings and throat-howkings.

It's still only nine o'clock.

The neighbour wakes up. Before, he'd only been a noisy mound. Now he's a burly young fellow with a weatherbeaten face. He asks me if I want the telly on. I say, no thanks. He tells me he's going out into the corridor to smoke a fag. If the doctor calls, I'm to say where he is. He's due out today.

There's more cloud in the sky now, shadows drifting along the ground. Birch branches trembling.

An auxiliary comes in to wash my feet, shave the hair on my right foot, cut the toenails very short, and paint the skin with iodine. While he's doing this, another auxiliary is sweeping the room. The sweeper pauses for a moment, looking at me hard:

'Excuse me, I don't want to bother you, but are you a singer?'

'A singer? No.'

'Well, there's a singer with the same name as you and who looks like you.'

'Is that so?'

'Are you sure you're not a singer?'

'Dead sure.'

At this, the foot-washer chips in to say:

'Maybe you'd like to be a singer.'

'Hell no, I've got better things to do.'

They move on to the next chore.

My neighbour comes back into the room. He's a fisherman. Eleventh generation of fisher folk, from Locquémeau: 'My section lies between Saint-Brieuc bay and Loctudy. I go in for scallops.' I say I'm from Trébeurden. 'The old guys of Trébeurden are a crafty lot,' he says with a laugh, referring to thefts of creels and tackle. He then asks me if it's the first time I've been operated on. I say, yes. Not him, he says, he's in and out all the time. And he shows me his leg, telling me it's got plastic in it, an accident on the boat. This time he was in to get a piece of glass cut out of his brow. He shows me it, now housed in a bottle. That was a car accident. It had nearly driven him off his nut. He's not just keeping it as a souvenir, he needs it, as proof for the insurance . . .

Around eleven, his family comes in, a young woman with two children, and he leaves with them:

'Kenavo!'

'Kenavo!'

Since I drink quite a lot of tea normally, and since I've drunk no tea at all this morning, I'm beginning to have a slight headache. I continue looking out of the window.

A man comes to the door. In a grey suit. With a tiny silver cross, I notice, in his lapel.

'Mind if I pay you a little visit?'

'Not at all.'

'I'm the almoner. What's the trouble?'

I tell him about my toe, and how I'm waiting for the surgeon.

'It's Dr Marquet, is it not?'

'I think so.'

'I really think it's him. He's very good. Everything all right?'

'Not bad.'

'Well, good luck.'

'Thanks.'

About a half-hour later, I get another visit. A guy in a white smock.

'Has your neighbour gone?'

'Yes.'

'Do you want to keep the telly?'

'No.'

He takes a key from his pocket, turns it in a lock on the machine.

'There we are,' he says.

I ask him if I'm still to be waiting long. He says he hasn't the faintest idea, he's 'exterior to the hospital'.

Time drags on.

About one o'clock, another auxiliary comes in to wrap up my foot in a big green napkin.

'I always like to make a nice parcel of it,' he says.

I lie there with my foot in the napkin, looking out the window, feeling my headache getting worse, smelling the stale guff from the ashtray . . .

At a quarter to three, a guy in a green smock comes to roll me to the operating block. We stop in the anti-chamber. I ask a woman: 'Can I have a word with the anaesthetist?'. She says: 'I'm the anaesthetist.' I show her the electrocardiogram Marie-Claude fished out for me. She glances at it, and hands me it back: 'No problem.'

I lie there in the anti-chamber.

A doctor comes in. Blue jeans, ill-shaven, puffing at a cigarette, which smells pretty strong in this confined space, and because of the fasting. The smoking medic talks with the anaesthetist and a nurse about yachts and then about some operation. I catch the words: 'I stuck the blade in and cleaned her up a bit.' I just hope he isn't part of the team. I'm glad to see him leave, taking his stinking fag with him.

At length, I'm rolled into the block.

A nurse asks me what my weight is (I think, why the hell didn't they ask me that before?), takes my blood pressure and sticks tabs on to my chest.

'You'll feel cold, then hot, and then things will begin to whirl.'

I feel the injection in my arm.

I don't feel cold, nor hot, and things aren't whirling, I just fade out . . .

Some time later, I can't say how long, there's a face bending over me, saying:

'Feel OK?'

My answer comes out of the depths:

'I was in Amazonia.'

It's only later I realise how strange it was to have said that. I had no specific images in my head, just a sensation of great amplitude.

I'm wheeled back to my room, and am told I'll be out next morning at eight.

I lie in bed, looking out of the window.

Marie-Claude comes to pay me a visit.

At eight o'clock, I'm given a light meal: white cheese, a yoghourt and a bowl of tea. The nurse says they can't give me much to eat. After the anaesthesia, you're liable to throw everything up.

During the night, nurses come in regularly to check my blood-pressure.

In the morning, I'm given tea, bread and butter.

Another nurse comes in:

'I've got the feeling I know you.'

'Yeah?'

'Do you do your shopping in Perros?'

'Nope.'

'Well, you've got a twin somewhere.'

'Maybe he's a singer?'

A few minutes later, I hear her, or another person at the counter in the corridor, saying:

'The artist's foot is on view!'

I look down at my foot, as if it wasn't part of me, but an independent pole of attraction.

The surgeon comes in, examines my toe, and says:

'That looks better.'

I'll have to be taking antibiotics. I'll have to be coming in regularly for dressings. He's taken out some mushed-up bone, but the toe should reconstitute itself. Everything should be OK.

The surgeon goes out. I keep lying there, with only one idea in mind: to get out into the freshness of the April morning, set my foot on the earth again, and have a few more looks at the world.

Why not Britain to start with?

Maybe it was time for me to renew contact with my native place, my home territory. Deep down, where it really mattered, I'd never actually lost touch – on the contrary, I'd extended it, expanded it over the years. But I thought it might be the moment to have a look around, say hello again . . .

Up through
Late Britain

I t was a gull perched on the Blackfriars' building that woke me up.

I got dressed and, leaving the inn where I'd spent the night, set foot on to the morning streets of Glasgow.

The Trongate clock marked 6.15. Only one or two people about. Blue sky, a bright day coming. I started to walk along Argyll street, then changed my mind and went down the Saltmarket. Still a fish-merchant there, and a shoeshop . . . Just a bit farther on, the Glasgow city mortuary. And then the Albert Bridge. Beyond the Albert Bridge, there used to be Gorbals Cross, and then the Gorbals themselves. But now, nothing. An emptiness. Another gull yelled: 'Welcome to the Void . . .'

I went back to my inn. Still nothing much doing there. Just a man sweeping the floor of the remains of last night's festivities. I'd come in around the midnight, and a couple of lads were giving it laldie with an Irish drum and a banjo. After thinking briefly of hanging about, I'd gone, dead beat, straight up to my room, where I'd fallen asleep right away.

'When's breakfast?' I asked the sweeper.

'Eight o'clock, Jim. Could make you a cuppa tea, if ye like.'

'No, no – no bother. I'll wait.'

And, going back up to my room, I lay down dressed on the bed with my hands clasped behind my neck.

Glasgow had changed. No doubt about it. It was cleaner, brighter, more spaced out. And yet an essential Glasgowness remained. In this inn, for example, with its photos of the city, the docks and old Glasgow characters, all round the walls . . .

I'd taken the train to Paris, and flown over from Orly to London.

'Like a newspaper?' said the driver of the taxi-cab that was taking me from Heathrow.

'No, thanks – I've got things on my mind.'

It was a quiet street, where the hotel was, The Anglia, and I was glad of that – till I got inside. There, it was like the Blitz. They were 'refurbishing' the entrance hall, and the noise was hellish. I was told I would not hear it on the fifth floor, in a room overlooking the courtyard. I didn't, true enough. But in the courtyard, a pneumatic drill was on the job. I sat there listening to the drill and looking at the Corby Trouser Service hung at the side of the bed. Then, casting off incipient depression, went down to Reception to ask for a quieter room. Nothing doing. Sorry. Just got to grin and bear it. Funnily enough, the idea of looking for another hotel simply didn't occur to me. Fatalism was setting in.

I went out for a meal.

Where to go?

Noise and heat in the ugly London streets.

I come across this place called *La Petite France*, and go in there. The *maître d'hôtel* is Spanish. The waiters are Italian. I tell the Spanishman I lived for years in Pau. 'Pau!', he says. 'I know eet.' And Biarritz, and St-Jean-de-Luz. I ask him how long he's been in London: 'Fifteen year – too long.'

I eat my fish, a rubbery bit of absolutely tasteless turbot with ninety-nine bones, then go back out into the streets.

Noise and heat.

I sat up, then, in the shade of my room, looking at the Corby Trouser Service, listening to the pneumatic drill, vaguely waiting for friends.

After a couple of hours, I went out to the Reception for news.

On coming out of the lift, I was surprised to see those friends of mine ensconced on a sofa. They'd been there for half-an-hour, slowly gathering dust.

How come I was so surprised? Hadn't I got their message?

No.

But they sent me a message.

The man at the the Reception checks. There is another White in the hotel. It was the other guy who got the message, and nobody will ever know what he did with it.

So, what's on the cards?

We're going out for a meal.

We go to an Indian's, down in a cellar, painted red, green and pink, picturesque little hole. And the waiter is a real hustler from New Delhi out to load England, Scotland, Ireland and Wales with the whole Himalayan menu:

'You like chapatti? . . . With some . . . And why not some . . . And some . . .'

It was some meal.

Roger told a story about the new place he'd bought in one of the heavy drug areas of London, up in Nottinghill, close by the Mangrove Club, and which he'd been converting into a studio – could hardly see your way to it through the clouds of marijuana smoke, and there were crack addicts and heroin heroes scattered all over the pavement. Mike recounted a recent trip to San Francisco he had made with his girlfriend and where they'd met ten local geniuses in the space of two days.

They both said London was all 'old stuff' now, nothing doing.

Right after breakfast the next day, I made for Euston station to take the train for Manchester.

Why Manchester?

There was absolutely no reason for me to go to Manchester, unless it was vague memories of Thomas de Quincey and the fact that Blake's *Ancient of Days* is in a museum there. It was just, I think, that I had never been there before. Anyway, it would be a quick-in, quick-out. Maybe what really interested me was just what I might see on and from the train.

On the concourse at Euston, I come across two big kiosques plunked right in the middle, the one selling socks, the other panties (this could only be England) and all round, food-counters and buffets. I go into one of the buffets, and sit listening to a beautiful-looking, sage-looking Indian at the next table explaining to an Englishman, who doesn't look too convinced, how *marvellous* life is, and how *astounding* it is they have met up again precisely here at Euston station and how he is sure the other will be a *great success* in his exciting new job, which is selling Dunkin Doughnuts.

In the train, I find myself sitting in a saloon-car with plush-pink seats like something out of a Victorian bordello, along with a dozen businessmen, the older ones with brylcreamed wavy hair, the younger ones more shorn.

A rabbit in a field . . . A travelling balloon . . .

Evening coming down over England.

Eight o'clock.

'This is the senior conductor speaking. We are arriving at Crewe. Passengers for Liverpool and Glasgow change here. Crewe station.'

And on we go.

To red-brick Manchester.

I check in at a hotel, then I go into town to look for dinner.

I don't eat the fish I'm served in the restaurant I come across. When I hand it back, the head-waiter doesn't even sniff it. He immediately offers to replace it with another dish. I force myself to down that other dish, just to fill my stomach.

And go back to my hotel. When you put the key in the lock, the metal plate falls off. When you turn on the shower you get a flow that wouldn't satisfy an anaemic ghost.

Next morning, after breakfast, I hastily consult a timetable and jump into a taxi for Manchester Piccadilly, intending to catch the 10.03 for Edinburgh.

No sign of any 10.03 to Edinburgh.

I ask a ticket-collector. He asks another ticket-collector. 'No 10.03 to Edinburgh, mate'. I go to General Enquiries. 'There's a 10.03 for Blackpool. You can get to Edinburgh by changing at Preston'. OK, great.

I go to the appropriate platform.

A lot of trains arriving and departing.

All late.

Loudspeaker booming:

'9.57. The train now arriving at platform three is the 9.43 from Liverpool, fourteen minutes late The train that will be arriving in two minutes at platform four is the 9.27 from Birmingham, thirty-three minutes late.'

It's easy to get a bit confused.

The first logical conclusion you come to is that if a train comes in on time, it can't be the right one.

Late Britain

Still keeping up appearances, though: the man who ushers the people on to the trains wears a top hat and tail coat.

'10.15. The train arriving at 10.18 at platform three will be the 10.03 for Blackpool'

A train comes in. I check: 'Blackpool' is written on its brow. I get on.

Off we go.

I hear the voice of the conductor giving a list of the stations we're to be stopping at.

No Preston.

Panic.

I lurch up to the top of the train, right up to the driver's cabin. The conductor's sitting beside him:

'Does this train stop at Preston?'

'Yoiss.'

'Will I get a train there for Edinburgh?'

There must be a slight trace of Celtic anxiety in my voice.

'You'll get a train there for Edinburgh, mate. Don't worry. We'll get you to Scotland OK.'

'Great – but when?'

'That I can't say. Don't have the timetable with me. But there'll be a train for you at Preston, mate, sure.'

Preston.

Huge empty station.

At least I'm glad to feel out of all the congestion and confinement.

I go into the station buffet and buy a packet of soft English sandwiches, eating them on the platform. I've checked: the train will be there in ten minutes. Everything, so far as I can ascertain, is under control.

After a few minutes, a voice announces that the train for Aberdeen will be twenty minutes late. I go and buy another packet of sandwiches.

In comes The Wolf of Badenoch.

That's the name of the train.

A tired wolf, limping in forty minutes late, but determined to drag itself to Caledonia or die in the attempt. I get aboard, with a light heart, and, I admit, a twinge of patriotism.

Entering the compartment, I see a red-haired Scottish businessman busy totting up figures on a sheet, a little lady all pink and frilly who turns out to be from Devon, and a young fellow with slanted eyes and jet-black hair, a long pale face and enormous glasses who is wearing a jerkin on which is written in startling letters:

MacBeth Sportsman's Club
Tokyo
Get the friends together

It's the Japanese, consulting a map, who breaks the silence:

'Where this train come?'

'Plymouth,' says the Devon woman brightly.

She's going on holiday to the Shetlands. Hopes there will be some sun. The train is running late, isn't it? The French trains are so much better, she says, they're always on time, and they look better.

'They're heavily subsidised,' retorts the Scotsman with punctilious authority. 'They can afford it.'

But the little Devon lady is right. The compartment *is* abnormally tatty. And everything is reduced to bottom level, with no pretence at anything like elegance. Every now and then a bloke passes by with a huge black plastic bag shouting 'Any refuse?'

Feeling thirsty, I make for the buffet. It's away up at the other end of the train. And when I get there, it's a sort of stall in a kind of cattle-waggon. I buy a can of beer, while a wee Scotswoman of about seventy, in buttocky slacks and with bobbed hair, asks primly for 'a measure of whisky'. I later hear her, in the compartment next to mine, telling somebody, and there may be a logic to it somewhere, that her father was a major in the Salvation Army.

Oxenholme. The Lake District. Trains to Kendal and Windermere.

'Looks just like the Cotswolds to me,' says the little lady from Devon.

Nobody takes her up on that.

Carlisle.

Carstairs.

This is where the train splits up. Front portion for Glasgow. Rear portion for Edinburgh and Aberdeen.

Beattock Summit.

I feel the big sweep of the land.

The Devon lady doesn't say it's just like the Cotswolds.

These circles of grey stone.

A lorry on the road: Norscot Seafoods.

This is it.

Nearing Edinburgh, we see a castle – or at least the Devon lady sees a castle.

'Is that Holyrood?' she asks.

'No, it's not Holyrood,' says the Scotsman.

'Which castle is it, then?' asks the Englishwoman.

The Scotsman reflects.

'I'm not sure,' he says. 'If I thought about it, I could probably work it out . . .'

He probably could too and I can see that, with Caledonian seriousness, he's going to try, even if it takes him all day, so I come to his rescue.

'There are so many of them up here,' I say.

'That's right,' he says, laughing. 'We only count the big ones.'

Coming out of Waverley Station, I made for Princes Street where I sat for an hour or two drinking coffee, contemplating the Scottish scene and listening to a bagpiper at the corner of the gardens, before making for the room I'd booked at the Caledonian Hotel.

I spent two days in Edinburgh, wandering up by Greyfriars (saying hello to the wee dog), and in the Cowgate (saluting my long lost Edinburgh cousins), looking up Robert Louis Stevenson at Lady Stairs House on the Mound, and taking a look into the map shop I used to frequent in the Canongate. I came across a beauty of a thing in there, a French seventeenth-century map, by Hubert Jaillot, of the *Costes d'Escosse*, that shows Scotland lying on its side as it were, with the north to the left of the map, and with the Western Isles, as far out as St Kilda, the *Isles Vesternes ou Inchgalles*, all clearly delineated. The whole west coast of Scotland was bathed in a smoky dark blue.

On the third day, I went up to Aberdeen on the Flying Scotsman:
The Forth Bridge.
Inverkeithing.
Aberdour.
Kinghorn.
Burntisland.
Kirkaldy.
Leuchars (for St Andrews).
Dundee.
The train was skelping and hurling along, hugging the shore, and my eyes were getting one sharp little image after another. Close at hand, the sea was pale blue, but darker on the horizon under a mass of grey-blue cloud. Then rain began to fall. And at Arbroath, sleet was lying on the ground.
Auchenblae.
Pitskelly.
Stonehaven.
A lighthouse there on the headland. A red tanker out in the grey stillness. And a yelling bevy of big fat-breasted Arctic gulls.

Aberdeen.

The Petrol Capital of Europe.

'Ay,' said the taxi-driver as he was taking me to the Northeastern Hotel, 'but everybody's beginnin' tae feel the bite. Ah can tell ye, away at the start, drivin' a taxi wiz like gettin' a licence tae print money. Ah'd get a bloke, a big high heid yin fae London, an' he'd say: "Take these men to Inverness, Edinburgh, Glasgow and Greenock." Ah'd get four full fares. Noo they're hirin' buses, an' they're no' comin' twice a week, they're comin' wance every three months. The boys wi' the sharp pincils are on the job. As to the lads on the platforms, aa they're waitin' for is the redundancy pension – the Golden Hashie they caa it.'

In the dining-room of the Northeastern that night, I could hear, amid pure Aberdonian ('We spent twenty thousand pounds refurbishin' it – any mair o' that wine left?'), the sing-songy monotony of Scandinavian, the breezy bluffness of Australian, and cool American-ese from California ('A real neat guy'). As for the *maître d'hôtel*, Luigi, from Lake Como, he must have the most excessively polite and pukka English accent north of Oxford.

The last time I was in Aberdeen, I was about thirteen years old, and it was on a summer holiday with my folks. Aberdeen seemed to me situated at the end of the earth, strange, solemn, dignified and cold. Now I'm wandering around like some Ishmael: Guild Street, Trinity Street, Union Street, going into bars offering 'Whisky, vodka, dark rum, gin' and, on Sundays, 'Exotic Girls', among earringed pirates in DMs and fargone oilrig zombies ('Three on, three off'), hearing about seals caught in plastic netbags, watching at midnight a morockless drunk buying himself a Smokey Bear Burger from a steamy van and, at three in the morning, those late June days, gulls gliding by my window as though on a 24-hour shift.

From Aberdeen, after a couple of days, I went to Glasgow, with which I started this erratic pilgrimage, and then I went down to Largs, on the west coast.

I'd thought of taking a hotel room in Fairlie, where I'd lived most of my youngest life, but I was afraid I might be recognised. I was on a reconnaissance trip, but I didn't want it to become over-personalized and encumbered. I wanted it to be a kind of *abstract* reconnaissance. What I did was take a hotel room in Largs, and from there I walked into Fairlie.

So I sat on a bench on the Bay Street in Fairlie, took a stroll down the Pier Road, stood on the Craigie Rock overlooking the village, and walked up the glen past black-faced sheep with drenched fleeces to the old rocks and trees covered with moss and lichen.

I still had the feel of all that. It's just that it wasn't so familiar.

Maybe better that way?

From my west coast hotel room at night, I could hear the tide rushing in over the stones of the beach. Walking along the waterfront in the daytime, you can hear it too. But it's in the background, with human voices in the foreground. Whereas at night, it's the tide-stone noise you have in the foreground, with human voices in the background.

I sat there in the west coast Scottish night, listening to the tide.

THE IRISH JAUNT

T he Irish jaunt was Kermarrech's idea.

Pol Kermarrech, my musician-neighbour of a few miles away, had lived in Ireland for six years, saying that he 'liked the country – with reservations'. As for me, I'd frequented it a little when I lived in the part-Irish city of Glasgow, but it had been some time since I set foot on it.

Pol set up a whole series of gigs: recordings, lectures and readings. We'd go all over the place and meet a lot of people.

We'd originally intended to cross by the night ferry from Roscoff to Cork, but, given our programme, it turned out to be more convenient to take the evening plane over from Paris to Dublin.

'Sky overcast – 11° Celsius', announced the Captain.

Sure enough, when we got into Dublin, the town was seeping in rain that bore a strong stench of coal smoke.

'God bless the house,' says I to myself.

A taxi took us over to O'Mara's place.

O'Mara, the fastest talker in the West, and who works at Radio Eirinn, already had the whiskey out, and the Tara Tinks, a music group, friends of the family, were just about to crack up a tune on banjo, fiddle and Irish drum. 'G,' says Paddy on the fiddle. Barney on banjo tunes up: 'Is that near enough?' Then the same Barney turns to the audience and says: 'This is a great tune – there are a lot of notes in it.' They played a lot of tunes, all with a lot of notes in them, and then I recited a poem about Brandan, with Barney interjecting every now and then 'Good, man', 'powerful', and Pol played a tune on the flute, and somebody else sang a song, and somebody else told a story . . .

It was the wee hours of the morning before I got to bed clutching in my hands a little note from a nice-looking Irish girl who hadn't been able to decide whether I was Franco-Scottish or Scoto-French (it's a nice point), which went like this: *'Monsieur! C'était une grand pleasure a dit bonjour a vous ce soir.'*

Next morning, which was a Saturn's day, with thick misty rain drifting along the Dublin streets and dripping through the forlorn leaves on St Stephen's Green (I thought I saw the ghost of James Joyce wiping his spectacles under a chestnut tree), I had breakfast with Pol, O'Mara and O'Mara's wife, Maureen, in a huge tearoom-restaurant.

The thing about this tearoom was the way all the waiters and the waitresses, all the cooks and the cookesses, were dressed. The man boiling the eggs had emerald green hair and a crimson ping-pong ball on his nose, while one of the waitresses sported flappy rabbit's ears and another wore a striped jersey, frilly knickers and football boots. I found it all a bit bizarre, but I kept my mouth shut. At length, though, probably seeing the tense questioning in my eyes, Maureen explained to me, soothingly, that it was Hallowe'en.

I was thereafter quietly enjoying my buns and tea when an old woman with bright eyes and a straggly mop of grey-yellow hair came up to our table and, addressing herself directly to me (there's another little mystery for you, how did she know I'd just come over from France?), said: 'Do you know what Oscar Wilde's last words were?' I said I regretfully did not. At which she proceeded to tell me that at that time Oscar was living in a room in a Paris hotel of which he didn't like the wallpaper, so he says to his friend: 'Either that wallpaper goes, or I go.' 'These were his very last words,' she continued, 'and it was he that went.' 'A worshipper of beauty to the last,' says I. 'Oh yes,' says she, and goes back to her table leaving me with the conviction that, despite all the politico-religious conflicts, all the ethical-metaphysical flapdoodle, all the literary flat-footedness, the respect for highflying writing and extravagant wit had not died out totally in Ireland.

At the French Institute in Dublin that night, I was to do a talk on 'intellectual nomadism'. I learned later that one of the professors at Trinity College had warned his students not to go to my talk since it would give them bad ideas, thus harming not only their souls but their careers. Just in case some students decided however not to take his warning, he'd sent a spy to keep things in order. In fact it was a very good crowd and the talk went well. But at question-time, up jumped this joker, fat and greasy, who, after a heatedly argumentative and improbably confused preamble, declared that I was 'making up my own scenario'. Since he was from the English department, I thought a nifty reference to T. S. Eliot would make him feel at home, so I told him that was what an 'individual talent' always did, but maybe I had been too provocative? 'You were not provocative at all!', he blustered. I said I was glad about that; it was just that he'd sounded provoked. He sat down, sweating, fuming and glaring.

Later again, during general conversation in the hall, a girl clamped on to me like a limpet and, despite all my efforts, just wouldn't let go. At length an older woman came up to me, her ever-loving mother, and wanted to know how long I'd known her. With a conscience crystal-clear, I declared that 'knowing' was a bit of an exaggeration, and, looking at my watch, said: 'twelve and a half minutes flat.' It turned out that the girl was coasting on some new transatlantic drug and had taken me for her long-lost brother from Heaven.

The following evening, I was at Radio Eirinn, where I had *carte blanche* and a full hour to express my ideas: about the Western tradition, Celtic culture, Europe, in fact anything I liked under the sun and even beyond it.

Pol was sitting at the recording table with the technician. At one point, as he went on turning the knobs and flicking the switches, this man murmured:

'Characters like that are dangerous. They shouldn't be allowed.'

'What do you mean?' said Pol.

'They're dangerous, I tell you. They should not be allowed.'

'In what way?'

'One of them wrote an article in the newspaper once.'

'Well, what of it?'

'My wife read it.'

'And?'

'She started going to evening classes.'

'So what?'

'She left me . . . Dangerous characters, I tell you, shouldn't be allowed.'

The morning of the next day, the Dublin streets were still full of coalsmoke-laden mist when we got into a car Pol still had in a garage (an old 4L he called 'The Goat') and set on the high road north. We had a date at a recording studio on the banks of the Carlingford.

So it was up by Slane, Ardee, Dundalk, Newry and down to Rostrevor on the Carlingford Lough, at the foot of the Mountains of Mourne.

At Check Point Charlie, where the South meets the North in an atmosphere of mutual distrust materialised by sten-guns and lines of sullen sand-bags, we were asked by a member of the Guard what we were going to be doing in the North. Pol, who knows the ropes, says: 'Oh, we're just going to be visiting some friends, officer.' The guard stalks round the car and takes a lingering look in the boot. 'Just visiting friends, is it?' 'Yes, officer.' With a curt nod and a laconic gesture, they let us through.

The Rands are a well-known musical family who recently bought this house on the Carlingford so as to gather the gang together. The recording studio is just across the yard. It was Colum Rand that was officiating there that day, and after they'd finished the recordings we went over to the house, where Colum's brother Tommy had just turned up from Belfast. Tommy's wife, who is French (Colum's is German), thereupon brought out the wine and the whiskey, and we had a singing and a talking night of it. Tommy sang his 'Round and round and up and down', and Colum sang his 'The man with the cap', and Pol sang a Breton song, *'Ar Gwezenn Avalou'*, the song of the apple-tree, and I almost sang 'The mountains of Mourne', but thought better of it (those guys were professionals), and just listened to Colum telling a story about windscreen wipers on the frontier between Switzerland and Germany during one of their concert tours. It was a long story with a wealth of detail, and I've forgotten the detail, but it all seemed very funny at the time. And funny stories are not Colum's speciality. He is a dour and silent character compared to his brother Tommy.

Tommy, then, told *his* story, a long rigmarolish shaggy-dog, endless and pointless affair, about the pink bath *Tonton*, their French uncle, a plumber to his trade, gave his wife and him as a wedding present. It was Tommy had had to reception it at the Dublin docks. So he went down there, saw a queue as long as an execution and waited in it like an effin' nitwit until he realised there was no reason on earth for him to be standing in that ticket queue. So he excused himself all round, and went right up boldly to the very top. 'What do you want?' said the man behind the window. 'I'm lookin' for a bath,' says Tommy. 'A *bath?!*' 'Ay,' says Tommy with his strong Northern accent, 'a bath, a pink bath, and I've got the measurements.' 'That sounds like Customs, if it's not the Loony Bin,' said the man. So Tommy went to the Customs. 'What do you want?' 'I want a bath.' 'Congratulations, but this is not the place.' 'Oh, but it is,' said Tommy, who had a letter in his pocket from *Tonton* and another letter from the port authorities telling him to come and pick up the bath *Tonton* had sent him as a wedding gift. He brought out these letters now. 'A pink bath?', said the man, perusing the documents carefully, even suspiciously. 'That's right,' said Tommy, still with his Northern accent. 'A wedding gift?', said the man. 'That's right,' said Tommy, brisk and sure of himself. 'From Europe?' 'That's right, from France.' 'This is going to take some time,' concluded the Southern man ponderously. It did. But Tommy finally got the massive pink thing into his van and, in case anybody should change his mind, was away with it like a shot to Rostrevor, where the pale-bloody object — I saw it with my own eyes — was installed, mission accomplished, with some ceremony.

And so to bed.

When I woke in the morning, it was to see the Carling fiord shrouded in mist, and it was easy to imagine a slim, grim Viking boat nosing its way along it, sniffing the soft Irish air . . . But there was no time to be wasted in historical revery, so we got The Goat out and beat it over to Sligo, where I was to salute the ghost of the last great poet to have come out of Ireland, and do a reading of my own stuff.

Into Sligo we slid, in a mauve light and a full moon shining over the

Silver Swan Restaurant, where we had a meal before making for the Yeats Centre.

After the reading, we were at the house of one of the Yeats Committee people, where we were to spend the night. The talk was about poteen (that's what we were drinking), about Boston, where the man of the house had lived for ten years: 'full of ultra-conservatives', he says, 'who haven't got into the twentieth century yet.' As to the woman of the house, she said she admired William Butler Yeats, of course, but she preferred the contemporary poets, because they were all 'family men' and talked about 'everyday concerns'. Since the notion of 'family poets' totally depressed me, I suggested some music. I know it's a *solution of facility*, but, well, life is sometimes very heavy. As it happened, the man of the house could sing in the old *sean-os* style, and Pol joined in with his skilful flute.

Next morning, Ben Bulben, that great brow of earth overlooking the wide Atlantic, was wrapped in a cold, rosy light and we went to Drumcliffe churchyard – the *crea-aak-ing* of the gate – to visit Yeats' tomb before climbing up Maeve's Hill in the mist, a great lump of a cairn from way back which no doubt contains the bones of Irish elks, woolly mammoths and other hyperborean creatures.

Back down in the twentieth century, we passed by the W. B. Yeats' Express Buffet and the Lake Isle Guest House, and penetrated via Tobercurry and Charlestown into the loch and mountain seaboard country of the beautiful and memory-laden (I'm thinking of my favourite old blind Raftery) County Mayo.

Castlebar.

Westport.

The shores of Loch Corrib.

Then it was swans and gulls by the mist-covered quais of Galway.

At Galway, I was to be doing a reading at a Poets' Club. This is the kind of gathering I strictly avoid. But Pol had assured me that Galway was considered as Ireland's number one avant-garde place, so I thought OK, let's have a look.

The meeting place was O' Flaherty's Pub, the time, nine o'clock. Pol and I were sitting there, on time and on our own, when the phone rang – for Mr Kevin White, which turned out to be me in a hibernian disguise. At the other end of the phone, which was hidden among green mountains of beer bottles in the back shop, was one Frances McNelly, telling me that it was she who'd been the guide at Yeat's Tower in Ballylee when it had just opened and which I'd been the first to visit, one chilly rainy day of over twenty-eight years ago . . .

At about nine forty-five, the members of the Poetry Co-operative Workshop began to drift in.

The leader was a German woman who declared that 'Ireland is a nation full of poetry,' and then went on to say that 'in this country at the present moment, are registered over five hundred poets'. 'That's quite a lot,' I said, feeling depression setting in again.

We then trooped up to the upstairs room where the Co-operative meetings are held, in the murky light of a candelabra and the heat of a tremendous arse-burning fire crackling in the grate. I went through with my reading, and after the reading there was a discussion. One woman says she's noticed I mention the sea a lot: 'I've always thought of the sea as a symbol of freedom,' she says. 'You don't say,' I say. Another said I referred to the East now and then and that she was interested in Japan. I said just a while back I had made a film in Japan with François Reichenbach, following the trail of Matsuo Basho. 'Is he still alive?' said the woman. 'Yes,' I said. Then it suddenly dawned on me she meant Basho . . .

I buggered off as soon as I decently could.

'I thought you said Galway was avant-garde', I said to Pol later in our hotel.

'Avant-garde for Ireland.'

The next morning we left for Cork, and got into it through a grey Atlantic downpour.

So there I was, and the rain falling in buckets, lodged by the River Lee in Moore's Hotel, which the local wags, no doubt with no real justification at all, call the Whores' Motel. What is sure is I saw no slinky lady from the lands of Limerick or Clare, but a big blowzy Stars and Stripes draped voluminously, if not voluptuously, on the landing of the stair as I went up, reminding you that Boston, I mean Irish America, is only a stone's throw away across the water. And from a newspaper picked up in the lounge I learned that a bunch of Irish kids in some village had just seen the Virgin Mary. There she was, walking down the High Street in front of the pub, in the flesh, every heavenly inch of her, in broad daylight, and twelve bonafide Irish children looking on. The local priests were sceptical, but the Vatican, being more up to date and publicity-conscious, was taking the affair very seriously.

That night I did a talk at the university of Cork about Celtic-born intellectuals who, over the centuries, have lived and worked in France.

And woke the next morning to a white mist full of gull-yells and a battered old sixpenny sun blinking over the river.

Pol and I took a quiet stroll down Crane Lane and Ship Street, then got back into The Goat, and returned up to Dublin.

On the Saturday following, we went down into Wicklow, where we gazed on quiet and lovely Glendalough: the blazing beeches, the red-berried holly and the green-golden pine, with smoke drifting over the glen and leaves dropping off the oak trees, before making for the coast at Arklow, where we spent the night.

It was raining early the next morning and I went for a walk on my own down the pier. Out in the misty waves there, under the rain, there was a lone grey heron, and it was that image I had mainly in my mind when we left Ireland, by the evening plane.

'What became of the kingdoms and the castles?, ends a Highland tale, 'I do not know. But I hope to hear more about them, next time I am out in the islands.'

Nowadays, we know all about the kingdoms and the castles, the republics and their squabbles. What we need is more news of the grey heron.

The grey heron at home in the grey rain.

A Trip to
the West Country

The West Country is all that territory that stretches out west of a line going from Bristol to Bournemouth: a long rocky peninsula full of bays and promontories, moors and valleys, that extends to the south-west and juts out vigorously into the Atlantic . . .

I'd left Roscoff in the rain, by the night ferry, but early the following morning, on the English coast, the sun was shining bright and along by the River Tamar the aspect of the countryside was idyllic: a slight frost still lying on the grass, but whin flowering, primroses and daffodils galore, winding little roadways lined with

Cornish hedges, farms offering *salad, fruit, cream,* lambs gambolling in the fields and gulls clamouring in the sky.

For long the River Tamar was a natural frontier. If the inhabitants weren't quite 'out of this world' there in the west, they were certainly out of England. It was the arrival of the railway, thanks principally to a Bristol engineer by the resounding name of Isambard Kingdom Brunel, that opened the country to civilisation. From that moment on it got labelled with the ridiculous title of 'English Riviera'. It is, of course, no riviera, but a Finisterrian Brittany. Here we're in the land of *pol, pen* and *porth* (I'm thinking of place-names), where Cornish, that Brythonic-Celtic language, was spoken up to the end of the eighteenth century.

Ten o'clock in the morning at Polperro, a little fishing harbour with white walls and blue shutters. No sound but the yelling of gulls and the gurgle of a stream that crosses the village. A sensation of freshness, a sense of peace . . . Then the doors begin to open. That of the restaurant The Merry Mackerel: 'Good morning, Mrs Fowey, lovely day!' That of a little bookshop with dusty shelves. Will I find on them John Davies's famous book about the 'mariner's secrets'?

There aren't that many fishing boats in the little harbour. That's because the great days of pilchard fishing have gone. But great days there were, and they remain strongly in the memories of the folk from Looe, Polperro, Megavissey. If pilchard fishing brought in such good returns, it was at least in part (economy sometimes works in mysterious ways) because of the Roman Catholic religion. Hence the toast that used to be proposed by Cornish fishermen in the taverns of the coast:

> *Here's a health to the Pope*
> *and may he repent*
> *and lengthen by six months*
> *the term of his Lent*

for it's always declared
betwixt the two Poles
there's nothing like pilchards
for saving of souls!

Fishing of a kind still goes on, of course, but on a small scale: for eels, cod, bream, whiting, crab and lobster. And then there's a big-time sports fishing – for shark, be it *mako, thresher, blue* or *porbeagle*. So if you want to come on like Hemingway in these parts, you can do so. But you may prefer to do like Dylan Thomas, who lived for a while on the coast here, at Newlyn, and who was content, between two poems, to invite the gulls to the window for breakfast.

If Cornwall was a land of sailors (in the Elizabethan Age, it was largely West Country lads who roamed over the ocean opening up new worlds), it was also a land of miners.

Cornish earth is rich in minerals, particularly copper and tin. And the region was known for this away back in the times of the Phoenicians, who would come up via Spain and Brittany to make trade with the islanders. Of Cornish mining life, little remains but traces: those old buildings with the high chimneys that dot the landscape. The fact is not only that the world market shifts, but that minerals run out. When the 'bad times' came to Cornwall, the miners left for other places – anywhere a mine would be opening, in the US, in Quebec, in Chile, in Africa, in Australia. Hence the saying: 'At the bottom of every hole in the earth, you'll find a Cornishman.'

Today, it's kaolin quarries that have replaced the mines. The backbone of the country is lined with great pyramids of grey-white dust known locally as 'the Cornish Alps'.

It'll come as no surprise that I decided to follow the coast.

At the beginning, I was travelling in the light of the spring sun, but before very long the whole coastal area was wrapped in mist. I found myself at Lizard Point, the southermost tip of England, the landmark for all those ships that used to round the coast of Spain and go along by Cape Horn before coming back again, as the old song says. Not a ship in sight. Only an enormous horn bellowing into the fog: two blasts followed by a long silence (but you could hear the sound groping its way through the fog . . .). The great black cliffs were sweating, as though they'd just made it out of chaos.

It isn't 'old England' you have here, even less modern England, it's archaic Albion.

I talk in his workshop with a stone-cutter, who works mainly with serpentine, one of the stones that constitute the Lizard's geological complex. 'Before radar', he says, 'there were a lot of wrecks in these parts.'

A good part of the Cornish population lived off those shipwrecks, as off smuggling. And it was difficult for a Cornishman to admit that there was anything illegitimate in either practice.

At Land's End later that day, the foggy mist was still about. Passing by as fast as possible the shops and Amusements that litter the place, I went down to see the waves. But I saw no wave. All I saw was a vague whiteness writhing and coiling in a greyness. And all I heard was the plaintive sound of another foghorn: this time, one note, regularly repeated.

It was while poking about a second-hand bookseller's in St Yves that I came across a book whose exaggeratedly alliterative title amused me: *Footprints of Former Men in Far Cornwall.* I'd bought it as a curiosity, thinking I'd have a look at it in some inactive moment. I'd have left it at that, but in the museum at Truro, lo and behold, didn't I come across the portrait of the man himself, I mean the author, R. S. Hawker ('sometime vicar of Morwenstow') and of one of the characters he talked about in his book, Black John the Dwarf. That's when my faintly pricked curiosity turned into a definite quest.

Morwenstow – I liked the sound of the name . . . A quick look at a map, and I'd found it: up there in the extreme north of Cornwall. I'd go and see.

But I was in no hurry.

At Zennor, I went up on to the moor (heather, wind, the far cries of curlews), looking for a strange dolmen called Zennor Quoit. I'm not sure I saw it – I must have passed by ten piles of rock that might have been it. But it really didn't matter. What I was really after was the moor itself.

So far as prehistory goes, I made up for lost time at Chysauster, a village inhabited from the second century before Christ to the second century after. I went up and down, and down and up, inspecting every detail. In the archaeological excavations, not a Roman coin was found, not a Roman object. It looks as if we have to imagine that those proto-Britishers lived completely outside history, be it Roman or Christian. For them, nothing but sun, rain, cattle, a field to be tilled, a little fishing, and the wind on the moor . . .

After that, I made for Tintagel, eager to see less the supposedly Arthurian fortress than the site itself.

It's in a pool on Bodmin moor that Arthur is said to have flung his good sword Excalibur. So no one will be surprised to see, plunked right in the middle of one of the cliffs of Tintagel, a bar bearing the name of Excali-bar. So much for the past. As for the future, it also has been taken in hand: there's another local institution called Amusement 3000.

In a pleasant inn at Bude (in the West Country, inn rooms can be like ships' cabins: heavy doors, black beams), while listening to bits of Country and Western music coming from the bar ('mother . . . raised him so well . . . now he's drinkin' in a honky-tonk an' raisin' hell'), I got down to reading Pastor Hawker's book: 'There is no part of our native country of England so little known as the middle moorland of old Cornwall [. . .]. Yet is there no scenery that can be sought by the antiquary or the artist that will so kindle the imagination or requite the eye or the mind of the wanderer as this Cornish solitude.'

When I get to the region of Morwenstow, the first thing I encounter is a Space Telecommunications Centre. But advancing further, I finally come across the old church of Morwenna, niched amid oaks and beeches, exactly as Hawker describes it in his book, the woody silence broken only by the black calls of rooks. And if you follow the cliff path, a marvellous landscape opens up before you: a broken coastline, with piles of fuliginous rock.

On one of those cliffs Hawker had built himself a little cabin made of driftwood. From it, he could contemplate the landscape and indulge in his own system of telecommunications by means of his cherished opium pipe.

The cabin is still there, as he left it. I took a seat in it, and spent a moment there, looking out over Tintagel to the south, and the isle of Lundy to the north, and in between, nothing – nothing but an expanse of blue emptiness all the way to Labrador.

I kept on my way.

In the lovely little village of Clovelly, whose streets are so steep that the inhabitants use sleds as a means of transport, I was sitting quietly on a bench in front of the Red Lion enjoying a mug of cider when two jets, followed right away by two others, split the sky with a hellish noise. On and on it went. Because of those damned contraptions, I left Clovelly faster than I'd intended and for a few kilometres I speeded up the rhythm of my trip. So I crossed Bideford and Barnstaple without stopping, with the idea of reaching Exmoor, as fast as possible, and the town of Minehead, where I'd thought of staying a while before going on into the Quantock Hills.

Minehead. As I turn right at the bottom of the avenue leading

to the shore, intending to stroll a while along the esplanade, I
come up against a 'leisure park': four huge installations entitled *The
Silver Dollar Amusement Centre, The Somerwest World, Showboat Amusements,
Carousel*, complete with fun pool, sunsplash, karts, mobikes and an
artificial sea equipped with islands, boats, pirates and sirens.
Enough to 'satisfy', I was informed, ten thousand people per
week . . .

I moved on.

On the whole, Exmoor is still preserved from all that glitzy nonentity.
Villages such as Allerford, Bossington, Selworthy, the little town of
Dunster, feel as if modernism has passed them by. As for the moors
themselves, the clear waters of the River Exe flow across them in
tranquillity, and on its banks I saw only one fisherman looking as if
he'd just stepped out of the pages of Mr Izaac Walton's little manual
of fishing and philosophy *The Compleat Angler*, which dates back to
1653.

And so I arrived at what is no doubt the most important place of
pilgrimage in all England: Glastonbury.

According to the legend, Christ personally set foot in these parts,
and if it wasn't the man himself, it was Joseph of Arimathea who
brought the Holy Grail with him. If you add to that the fact that in
the twelfth century the local monks claimed they had unearthed the
coffin of, guess who, right, King Arthur, you see how much collateral
there was to attract visitors.

In our day, it's the representatives of the New Age you find here in
hordes, with the Bible in one pocket, the *I Ching* in the other, and in
their heads an improbable hash. While a soothsayer calling herself
'the Witch of Salem' predicts the future, a guy with his face painted
green chants hymns from the Veda . . .

I don't hang around very long.

What I do is make off for the megaliths of West Kennet, and the

remains of the old 'Wessex culture': that amber from the Baltic, those
necklace beads from Egypt, those bronze pins from Bohemia found in
the tombs of Wiltshire.

I'm thinking of this 'Wessex culture' and this archaic Europe as I make
my way to Dorchester, in Dorset, to pick up the tracks of Thomas
Hardy.

It was no doubt Hardy, in that series of books he called 'the
Wessex novels', who gave this land its fullest expression, giving life to
characters that incarnate its complex energies and hence don't fit
easily into society.

I'm thinking in particular of *Far from the Madding Crowd*.

The very title rubs some people the wrong way. But others, their
numbers probably on the increase, see in it a vision of things and hear
in it an accent they've been in want of for a long time.

What is striking about Hardy's books is not the inventivity of the
story- teller's art (others can do that just as well), it's the macroscopic
and microscopic vision of things contained in them. I'd go even
further. With Hardy, everything in humankind that is invention,
whether it be on the material or the spiritual plane, has to take second
place to discovery of the world, and, in his books, all that is
romanesque (intrigue, melodrama, human imbroglio) is as nothing
compared to the silent world around: events are lost in eternity,
minds mingle with the land. I'm thinking, for example, of the second
chapter of *Far from the Madding Crowd*, which gives the fundamental
tone to the whole book. It's 20 December, at midnight, a 'desolate'
wind is blowing from the north, and the shepherd Gabriel Oak is
watching over his sheep on Norcombe Hill, one of those places that
seem 'indestructible', open to cosmic space and marked by a 'grey
simplicity'. Gabriel is on the watch there alone, between earth and
sky, listening to the noise of the wind on the grass and in the trees,
and gazing up at the stars. His physical and mental concentration is
such that he can almost feel in his body the movement of the earth.

It's only after this moment of cosmic consciousness that the story really begins. There's always a story, history is always there, but, for Hardy, the fundamental and the essential are elsewhere.

Thomas Hardy's world is a world with no ideal (but not without intense life-images), without hope (but not without living presence), without sentimentality (but not without elementary sensation). Some said in his day he was pessimistic, even inhuman. He would say in reply that he was concerned neither with optimism, nor pessimism, nor meliorism, just with truth. That attitude went along with a certain disillusionment, or let's say, with a certain desidealisation, and the return to fundamental ground. Hardy's three great books, *Jude the Obscure*, *The Return of the Native* and *Far from the Madding Crowd*, constitute a trilogy of disillusionment, rediscovered density and austere joyance.

In a poem, 'Afterwards', he wrote this:

> *If, when hearing that I have been stilled at last, they stand at the door,*
> *Watching the full-starred heavens that winter sees,*
> *Will this thought rise on those who will meet my face no more,*
> *'He was one who had an eye for such mysteries'?*

The word 'mysteries' is too much for my taste, but no matter, I can go along with the general tenor.

After following Hardy's tracks in Dorchester itself (the ex-owner of the Antelope Hotel tells me how Hardy liked to come in for a beer in the morning, listening to the conversations) and at Stinsford, where as a child he went to church, I went on a little pilgrimage to his birthplace at Little Bockhampton, a cottage built by his grandfather at a secluded spot surrounded by wood and moor.

In the garden, a blackcurrant bush in flower gave out an unfathomable perfume . . .

After that, it only remained for me to move along the coast to Exeter, cross Dartmoor in the rosy mists of evening, reboard the *Quiberon* at Plymouth, and go back to the labours and the loves of my Breton hermitage.

Kenneth White
The French bibliography
(only mainline books listed)

Prose narrative

Les Limbes incandescents, translated from the English by Patrick Mayoux, Paris, Denoël, Les Lettres nouvelles, 1976. New edition, Paris, Denoël, 1990.

Dérives, several translators, Paris, Laffont, Lettres Nouvelles/ Maurice Nadeau, 1978.

Lettres de Gourgounel, translated by Gil and Marie Jouanard, Paris, Presses d'aujourd'hui, 1979. New edition, Paris, Grasset, Les Cahiers rouges, 1986.

L'Écosse avec Kenneth White, Paris, Flammarion, 1980. New edition, Arthaud, 1988.

Le Visage du vent d'Est, translated by Marie-Claude White, Paris, Les Presses d'aujourd'hui, 1980.

La Route bleue, translated by Marie-Claude White, Paris, Grasset, 1983. Prix Médicis étranger. Livre de poche no. 5988.

Les Cygnes Sauvages, translated by Marie-Claude White, Paris, Grasset, 1990.

Corsica, l'itinéraire des rives et des monts, translated by Marie-Claude White, Ajaccio, La Marge, 1999.

Poetry

En toute candeur, bilingual edition, translated by Pierre Leyris, Paris, Mercure de France, 1964.

Mahamudra, le grand geste, bilingual edition, translated by Marie-Claude White, Paris, Mercure de France, 1979.

Le Grand Rivage, bilingual edition, translated by Patrick Guyon and Marie-Claude White, Paris, Le Nouveau Commerce, 1980.

Scénes d'un monde flottant, bilingual edition, translated by Marie-Claude White, Paris, Grasset, 1983.

Terre de diamant, bilingual edition, translated by Philippe Jaworski, Marie-Claude White and the author, Paris, Grasset, 1983.

Atlantica, bilingual edition, translated by Marie-Claude White, Paris, Grasset, 1986. Prix Alfred de Vigny.

Les Rives du silence, bilingual edition, translated by Marie-Claude White, Paris, Mercure de France, 1997.

Limites et Marges, bilingual edition, translated by Marie-Claude White, Paris, Mercure de France, 2000.

Essays

La Figure du dehors, Paris, Grasset, 1982. Livre de poche, Biblio essais 4105.

Une apocalypse tranquille, Paris, Grasset, 1985.

Le Poète cosmographe, interviews, Presses universitaires de Bordeaux, 1987.

L'Esprit nomade, Paris, Grasset, 1987.

Le Monde d'Antonin Artaud, Bruxelles and Paris, Éditions Complexe, 1989.

Hokusaï ou l'horizon sensible, Paris, Terrain Vague, 1990.

Le Plateau de l'Albatros, introduction à la géopoétique, Paris, Grasset, 1994.

Le Lieu et la Parole, interviews, 1987–1997, Cléguer, Éditions du Scorff, 1997.

Les Finisterres de l'esprit, Cléguer, Éditions du Scorff, 1998.

Une stratégie paradoxale, essais de résistance culturelle, Presses universitaires de Bordeaux, 1998.

Le Chemin des crêtes, avec Stevenson dans les Cévennes, Esparon, Études et Communications, 1999.

Latitude atlantique, Quimper, Editions Palantines, 2000.